Reimagining the future

towards democratic governance

Reimagining the future

towards democratic governance

A report of the Global Governance Reform Project

Project directors and sponsoring institutions

Joseph A. Camilleri
The Department of Politics, La Trobe University, Melbourne

Kamal Malhotra
Focus on the Global South, Bangkok

Majid Tehranian
The Toda Institute for Global Peace and Policy Research, Tokyo and Honolulu

Printed and Published in Australia
© The three project directors, 2000

National Library of Australia
Cataloguing-in-Publication entry:

Camilleri, J.A.; Malhotra, K.; Tehranian, M.
Reimagining the future: towards democratic governance

Bibliography
ISBN   0 646 39994 2

1. International organisation. 2. Globalization. I. Malhotra, Kamal. II. Camilleri, J. A. (Joseph A.), 1944- . III. Tehranian, Majid. IV. La Trobe University. Dept. of Politics. V. Focus on the Global South. VI. Toda Institute for Global Peace and Policy Research. VII. Title.

341.2

Front cover design by Adrian Carson Design
Layout and design by Vista Publications
Printed by Arena Printing and Publishing
Published and distributed by
       The Department of Politics, La Trobe University
       Bundoora Victoria 3083 Australia
       Telephone: 61 3 9479 2287
       Fax: 61 3 9479 1997

Contents

Contributors to the project

Working Group members

Esref Aksu
Department of Politics, La Trobe University, Melbourne

Professor Joseph Camilleri
Department of Politics, La Trobe University, Melbourne

Professor Stephen Gill
Department of Political Science, York University, Toronto

Ehito Kimura
Previously with Focus on the Global South, now studying at Yale University, New Haven, CT

John Langmore
Director, Division for Social Policy and Development
Department of Economic and Social Affairs, United Nations, New York

Kamal Malhotra
(on leave of absence from Focus on the Global South)
Senior Advisor, Civil Society Organizations and Participation Programme
Bureau of Development Policy, UNDP, New York

Marco Mezzera
Focus on the Global South, Bangkok

Professor Kinhide Mushakoji
Meijigakuin University, Yokohama

Olle Nordberg
Director, Dag Hammarskjöld Foundation, Uppsala

Professor Majid Tehranian
University of Hawaii at Manoa, and Director, Toda Institute for Global Peace and Policy Research, Tokyo and Honolulu

Professor Shibin Yuan
Foreign Affairs College, Beijing

Eminent Persons Advisory Group members

Dr Boutros Boutros-Ghali
Secretary-General, Organisation Internationale de la Francophonie, Paris

Gareth Evans
President, International Crisis Group, Brussels

Professor Richard A. Falk
Center of International Studies, Princeton University, Princeton, NJ

Dr Noeleen Heyzer
Director, UN Development Fund for Women (UNIFEM), New York

Dr M. Javad Zarif
Deputy Foreign Minister, Islamic Republic of Iran

Others who have contributed papers, advice or organizational support

Professor George Andreopoulos, *The Graduate Center, The City University of New York*

Dr Henk-Jan Brinkman, *Development Policy Analysis Division, Department of Economic and Social Affairs, United Nations, New York*

Dr Valerie de Campos Mello, *Office of the Under-Secretary-General for Political Affairs, United Nations, New York*

Dr Kevin Clements, *General Secretary, Alert International, London*

Professor Juergen Dedring, *The Graduate Center, The City University of New York*

Sophie Theven de Gueleran, *UN Intellectual History Project, New York*

Associate Professor Michael Hamel-Green, *Department of Social Inquiry and Community Studies, Victoria University of Technology, Melbourne*

Adam Harmes, *Department of Political Science, York University, Toronto*

Harish Iyer, *New York*

Dr Tapio Kanninen, *Chief, Policy Planning Unit, Department of Political Affairs, United Nations, New York*

Audrey E. Kitagawa, *New York*

Fr Paul Lansu, *Pax Christi International, Brussels*

Randall Larsen, *University of Hawaii at Manoa, Honolulu*

Andrew Mack, *Director, Strategic Analysis Unit, Executive Office of the UN Secretary-General, New York*

Rik Panganiban, *World Federalist Movement, New York*

Gay Rosenblum-Kumar, *Department of Economic and Social Affairs, United Nations, New York*

Hiro Sakurai, *UN Representative, Soka Gakkai International, New York*

Dr Hamid Shirvani, *Vice-President, Queens College, The City University of New York*

Professor Thomas G. Weiss, *The Graduate Center, The City University of New York*

Dr Susan Wright, *Department of History of Science, University of Michigan, Ann Arbor, MI*

Foreword

Boutros Boutros-Ghali

Democracy is a major and immediate concern for our world today and extending democracy at the international level – that is democracy beyond borders – is not utopia. It is the challenge of the next decades.

The two most important legacies of the last years of this century are the end of the Cold War and the acceleration of process of globalization. The nuclear confrontation between West and East, between capitalist democracy and Soviet communism is past history. The globalization of economic, social and cultural life is a continuous process and future generations will have to come to terms with it even more than the present generation. Our responsibility is to look beyond the crises of the moment and to help prepare the world community for the problems and opportunities of the future.

Today, the international community is anxiously searching for a new global political balance. For some, the ideal would be an international system in which a few hundred multinational companies and a few big powers could negotiate deals designed to further their own interests. Some others would prefer global technocratic solutions. I hope that the leaders of tomorrow will totally reject these approaches. We must fight to establish new interstate relations based on the democratization of the family of nations. Hence the need to extend the concept of democracy to the global level.

Democracy can no longer be limited to the nation-state. The democratization of international relations will require creation of new political institutions or the transformation of the existing international organizations, which will coexist with the system of nation-states but which would overrule states in certain spheres of activities which require global regulations.

How can we contribute to the democratization of the family of nations? Greater involvement of states in world affairs, the reform of the UN Security Council, the reform of the UN Economic and Social Council, increased participation of regional organizations, a new role for the civil society, for the NGOs, more involvement for parliamentarian and local authorities, participation of business and industry, more involvement of the media, these are the key issues in the debate on the democratization of the international society.

The authors of this study, through an original approach, help us to formulate imaginative, yet realistic proposals for change. They should be thanked for having launched this debate at such a high level. It is now our common responsibility to contribute to the development of this global governance concept. And let me believe that what is utopia today may be reality tomorrow.

Richard A. Falk

As the Cold War recedes from active political consciousness, there is a growing sense of restiveness about how the world is organized, and where human society is heading. Fundamental to this discomfort is the perception that capital-oriented economic forces have gained control over governmental policy-making at all levels of social organization, but especially at the level of the state. Without any formal authorization, the World Economic Council at Davos that brings together mega-capitalists on an annual basis has virtually displaced the United Nations as a source of guidance on global issues. In this economistic setting, where trade, investment, and economic growth are the prime focus of dominant political trends, there is an ironic climate of opinion that wierdly resembles the Marxist/Leninist insistence that political life is necessarily a passive reflection of the economic interests and ideology of business and finance. Such an unwitting assimilation of a Marxist outlook by world capitalism in this era of globalization could not have been anticipated, and has yet to be properly understood as a kind of strange afterglow left behind by the collapse of Communism as a world political force.

Against such a background, *Reimagining the future*, is a remarkable achievement: bringing to consciousness a comprehensive understanding of how to revive political life on a global basis, accompanied by a creative reformulation of a people-oriented menu of priorities for the global policy agenda. What distinguishes this report is its combination of conceptualizing democracy for a world order in which territorial orientations are being superseded with an array of concrete proposals for global reform that will embody ideas and values in innovative structures of governance, especially in relation to the United Nations System. An integrated course of action for transnational social forces is presented that is at once sophisticated in its analysis, and yet easily accessible to anyone concerned with global change.

Such a presentation contributes to an emergent sense that a movement of resistance and reform within global civil society is beginning to take shape before our eyes. This impression was also fostered by 'the battle of Seattle' in which dramatic street protests overshadowed the World Trade

Organization formal meetings by mounting a militant challenge to the fundamental claims of neo-liberal globalization. But to convert an unsettling challenge into a robust political program for reform depends on developing ideas and a coherent overview that are responsive to the specifics of the global setting. This is precisely what this study does so brilliantly, and with a technical mastery that makes its blend of theorizing and recommending so indispensable for activists and reflective citizens.

By concentrating on global governance, financial flows, and peace and security, *Reimagining the future* provides a framework for thought and action that integrates the many focused and distinct undertakings heretofore associated with transnational and local political activism. This is an important contribution at a time when a transformative politics of global scope needs to confront neo-liberal globalization with an alternative way of conceiving the future that is comparably coherent. It must also be capable of absorbing into its worldview issue-oriented perspectives associated with human rights, environmental protection, women, debt relief, institutional reform, and disarmament. The banners of 'global democracy' are being unfurled here as a unifying rallying cry to the peoples of the world. It presents as global democracy this quest for effective modes of accountable governance that are humane, dedicated to the alleviation of suffering, and genuinely committed to achieving a far more equitable and participatory sharing of the potential benefits for human well-being of information technology. Of course, this is a tall order, but do the requirements of the age for peace, justice, security, and serenity demand any less?

A final observation: the authors of this study, and their sponsoring organizations, are situated in the Asia-Pacific region. This common point of origin gives this entire project a refreshing detachment from the standard preoccupations of Europe and North America, and unconsciously offers the world a non-hegemonic way of conceiving global governance. This is not a trivial matter. So much of prior world order thinking, even when it purports to be counter-hegemonic, is coloured by its locus within the Euro-American power centres, thereby implicitly undervaluing the creative potential of other cartographies of power, influence, and imaginative action, and not deeply engaging those with the greatest incentive to engage in the struggle for global reform. Here, at last, is a global strategy developed in an Asia-Pacific setting from which we in the West can learn, including the humbling realization that others may have better answers to the dilemmas of our time than we have!

Noeleen Heyzer

The United Nations has played and continues to play a crucial role in the establishment and implementation of global norms for the economic, social and political rights and security of people throughout the world. I welcome this publication, which, while it is understandably critical of what has been achieved so far, has constructively and imaginatively proposed ways of democratising and strengthening our future collective governance.

Through a series of world conferences and the ensuing agenda for action, the United Nations has succeeded in raising the world's consciousness on issues that are of global importance. Today's world is shaped by three major phenomena: economic globalization; fragmentation; and vulnerabilities without borders. Economic globalization, while generating new opportunities, has been accompanied by many costs, including inequality, social exclusion, and the concentration of wealth in fewer and fewer hands. Social and political fragmentation along social and ethnic lines has led to a surge in intra-state conflicts and mounting insecurity. The proliferation of criminal networks, the spread of infectious diseases, notably as HIV/AIDS, and the alarming destruction of the environment are among some of the problems that transcend national borders, and exceed the problem-solving capacities of any single actor.

At the same time, the world has seen a surge in the numbers and types of non-state players emerging on the world stage to undertake an increasingly significant role. Such non-state actors include regional institutions, parliamentarians, the media, a host of civil society organisations and the private sector. More than ever before, there is a need to increase our common understanding and to highlight the shared responsibility required for the creation of a more coherent and responsible international community based on the consensus, conventions and treaties of the United Nations.

The demands being placed on the United Nations are continually expanding while its resources are shrinking. Reforming the UN system and democratizing the broader system of global governance to enable it to respond to changing realities will require more than a focus on greater efficiency. As this publication indicates, it will necessitate a commitment of significantly greater resources and power to the United Nations, and the inclusion of non-state actors, especially organised civil society, in its functioning. It will also require more inclusive regional arrangements which enhance pluralism in ideas and proposals that are so crucial to democratic governance.

This publication, which offers us such an array of realistic proposals and ideas, makes a positive contribution to both envisioning and realizing a more democratic and secure future for states, nations and communities. While a world where all women and men enjoy equality, peace and continuing development is a vision which the authors of this publication share with the United Nations system, they are right to remind us how far we still have to travel if this vision is to become a reality.

─────────────────

Mohammad Javad Zarif

We have put behind a century, which was characterized by unprecedented progress in science and technology, improving the living conditions of mankind, albeit in an uneven manner, and providing even greater untapped potential, which is yet to be collectively utilized for the equitable and sustainable development of all members of human family. At the same time, the twentieth century was marred by a legacy of unparalleled destruction of human beings and their physical and natural environment, caused by advancement of weapons of mass destruction, coupled with wanton disregard for human life and the environment.

As we enter a new millennium during a transitional period in international relations, humanity has a unique opportunity to devise new and more humane approach to governance at the national as well as global levels. The fluid nature of the post-polar world provides a breathing space for articulation and formation of universal consensus around innovative and imaginative ideas and initiatives, which can and must break with outdated, yet predominant, perceptions and paradigms.

A reform in governance requires, first and foremost, a reform in prevailing mentalities and the dominant paradigm governing human interactions. The paradigm of interaction and governance in the twentieth century could probably be best characterized by the phenomenon of exclusion: exclusion of actors as well as ideas. The dominant interests of the Cold War era necessitated a world conception based on rivalry and block formation. Thus, governance required enemies, and security and even prosperity were at one time or another perceived as zero sum propositions. The fallacy that security or prosperity for one group could be achieved at the expense of another fuelled the arms race, coercion and exploitation. Nations, cultures and ideas were also measured in terms of their conformity with certain dominant assertions; assimilation or isolation and demonization were the only choices.

Furthermore, the paradigm of exclusion left the entire group of non-state actors outside international decision-making and value distribution processes. While the role and contribution of civil society organizations, academia, intellectuals and thinkers has recently received increasing recognition and appreciation in the global scene, their role, particularly in the international peace and security debate, continues to be marginal at best.

It is indeed encouraging to note that the valuable and imaginative studies and recommendations prepared for the Global Governance Reform Project address a good number of these inherent deficiencies of the paradigm of exclusion. Transparency, collective co-operation, empowerment and participation, tolerance and understanding in deliberations and decision-making processes within global multilateral institutions together with the prevalence of solid accountability have been wisely identified as major requisites which would contribute enormously to establish a democratic and more humane governance at the global level. I submit that this report, by addressing the paradigm itself explicitly, and developing these and similar principles and initiatives, offers us useful building blocks for a new paradigm and modality of relationships based on inclusion.

The new approach based on inclusion rests on not only respect for, but indeed celebration of diversity. Contribution together with mutual enrichment of all cultures and civilizations, states and non-state actors as well as individuals should not be merely welcomed but need to be regarded as indispensable. Furthermore, the fundamental change in perception that is the prerequisite for a change of paradigm would entail fundamental revision of current global security and development policy. 'Global security networking' would replace block rivalry and zero-sum security doctrines, providing a more conducive environment for disarmament and peacemaking; and balance and equitable human development would become the prevailing concern in formulation of global trade, finance and monetary arrangements. A reformed United Nations will have the primary role in forging global consensus on various challenges facing the current and future generation. The enhanced participation of thinkers, intellectuals, academia and civil society organizations, and most importantly the youth, in articulating as well as supervising an appropriate response to these challenges, would ensure fairness and greater accountability coupled with more serious collective consideration of our common future.

The initiative of President Khatami, in his capacity as Chairman of the Organization of the Islamic Conference, to launch a global campaign for dialogue among civilizations, represents an attempt to seize the moment of global transition and to instil a new modality of interaction based on dialogue, understanding and inclusion of all. The positive reception of this suggestion by the United Nations, and the designation of the first year of the new millennium as the United Nations Year of Dialogue among Civilizations is one indication that the world might after all be ready for such a fundamental and historic change in orientation.

Preface

Countless words have been spoken and written on the subject of UN reform — so far, it seems, with little effect. Can we seriously expect more words to succeed where so many others have failed?

This more than any other question has concentrated our minds over the last three years. In examining the evolving global multilateral system, we have been struck by the numerous and often conflicting interpretations of the scope and limitations of institutional change. Not surprisingly perhaps, UN reform has come to mean different things to different people. For some, it means greater administrative competence; for others, downsizing of various kinds; for others still, less interference in the internal affairs of states.

For this project the main preoccupation has not been the efficient use of resources, or the speed with which decisions are made, highly desirable though both may be. Nor has it been the reorganization of this or that arm of the UN system, necessary though this undoubtedly is. Rather, our approach has been to rethink the puzzle of global governance by placing it squarely within the context of a globalizing economy.

This larger canvas, we are persuaded, offers the only appropriate analytical framework. It sheds new light on the present institutional fabric of international society and on its future possibilities. It widens our intellectual horizons and at the same time enhances our capacity for sustained initiative. This project, the first results of which appear in this publication, is therefore concerned first and foremost with meeting the challenges of globalization, with all that this implies for human security. Simply put, its focus is the legitimacy of the emerging system of global governance.

When most people hear the word 'globalization' they often think of a set of mega-trends and processes creating a more interlinked and integrated world. Phrases like 'the global village', 'the information society' and 'one world, ready or not!' all convey the impression of a massive historical process that is beyond human control. Governments, economies and social institutions, we are told, have no alternative but to adapt to these apparently inexorable forces.

Plausible though it may sound, this view of the world is dangerously simplistic. It conveniently forgets that globalization is not just a set of trends, but also a conscious political project. Global capital and technology flows are not divinely preordained, they are the result of conscious decisions and policies.

Of course, 'globalization' is many-faceted and multidimensional. It involves ideas, images, symbols, music, fashions and a variety of tastes and representations of identity and community. Yet such diversity and complexity cannot obscure the fact that the world's productive assets and the world's trade and financial markets are now dominated by large institutional investors and transnational firms.

As a consequence we have seen the commercialization of almost every facet of social interaction: family life, religious practice, leisure pursuits and even aspects of nature. Increasingly, patent rights over human genes and tissue, plants, seeds and animal hybrids, and even the DNA of 'endangered peoples'– that is, aboriginal or native peoples – are routinely acquired by pharmaceutical and agricultural corporations. These private 'intellectual' property rights are being internationalized and extended into the legal regimes of the world, in particular through the new World Trade Organization. Such developments are gathering pace in much of the OECD, even though little mainstream political debate has yet occurred on the repercussions of biotechnology and genetic innovation, to say nothing of the privatization of life forms.

To put it crudely, globalization from above, or what Richard Falk has labelled 'predatory globalization' may be interpreted as an attempt to defend patterns of privilege from encroachment and possible expropriation by those subordinated and marginalized. Contemporary systems of policing and military power, not least the use of force in the 1991 Gulf War and later NATO's military assault in Serbia/Kosovo, are manifestations of this defensive strategy.

The dominant form of globalization is therefore best described as the deepening and extension of the mutually-reinforcing power of transnational capital and the G7 states on a world scale. Such power is economic but also political, military, juridical and cultural. It encompasses the OECD countries but also much of the former Soviet bloc and the Third World. As Stephen Gill has argued, the ensuing restructuring of economies, polities and societies has helped to create a 'constitution for global capitalism', which seeks to harmonize the legal structures of disparate states into a global quasi-constitutional structure of laws, rules, regulations and standards. Its principal function is to consolidate the privileged consumption and production patterns of a small section of the world's population.

If the notion of global governance is to do justice to the multiple challenges of globalization, then multilateral reform cannot be confined to the United Nations. To reform the Secretariat and its various departments – or even the Security Council and the General Assembly – is important but clearly not enough. Needless to say, the UN's specialized agencies, programmes and commissions are all an integral part of the reform agenda. But so are the world's most powerful international institutions, notably the WTO, the World Bank and the IMF, which ironically enough have only the most tenuous links with the UN's principal deliberative organs.

Nor can the fate of multilateral institutions be divorced from the actions of their member states or of other actors on the world stage. Writing more than a decade ago, Sir Sridath Ramphal, then Commonwealth Secretary-General, observed:

> the paradox and tragedy of recent times is that even as the need for better management of relations between nations and for a multilateral approach to global problems has become more manifest, support for multilateralism has weakened, eroded by some of the strongest nations... This is most true, of course, of the United States, whose recent behaviour has served actually to weaken the structures of multilateralism, including the United Nations itself.
>
> Harrod and Schrijver (eds), *The UN under Attack, 1988*

Much that has happened since the end of the Cold War has confirmed the accuracy of this assessment. There can be little doubt that the United States in particular and the five permanent members of the Security Council more generally have often allowed narrow self-interest to dictate their actions. Whether by omission or commission, they have tarnished the UN's reputation, and with it the appeal of international citizenship. Yet, they are not the only culprits.

Rwanda, Somalia, East Timor, Sierra Leone, to name a few, are living reminders of the short-sightedness of states, large and small. The inadequacies of international bureaucracies are numerous and well known. But more significant is the role of large TNCs, banks and financial markets. The enormous, often highly damaging, impact of their decisions is matched only by an almost complete lack of accountability, except perhaps to their shareholders, and indirectly at best to their customers. The failure of the media to inform and analyse accurately and impartially is itself highly damaging to any prospect for humane governance. Nor can NGOs, especially some of the larger ones, be regarded as entirely blameless, if one is to judge by their petty rivalries, the priority often given to protecting their own turf, and their frequent failure to consult with the people whose needs are ostensibly their primary concern.

In the face of these institutional bottlenecks, it is time to return to first principles. This is not to dismiss the usefulness of incremental change, or the need for practical reforms. On the other hand, a return to first principles is itself a practical necessity. Without it, it is hard to see how states, peoples and the international community generally will renew their enthusiasm for reform, or indeed how they will oversee, over a prolonged period, the small but innumerable legal, administrative and financial steps that are needed along the way.

This project takes, then, an unashamedly radical perspective – not in the sense that it makes revolutionary proposals, but that it keeps the spotlight on a number of fundamental questions:

- Is it possible to democratize the global (and regional) multilateral system? If so, how? Is democratization compatible with effectiveness and traditional notions of sovereignty?

- Are security and economy separate concerns? If not, how can the necessary connections be made, conceptually and organizationally?

- Is it true that we are seeing the early signs of an emerging global civil society? If so, is such a movement to be encouraged? By what practical steps? Can civil society organizations contribute more effectively to global governance? With what consequences for global multilateral institutions?

The authors of this study are of the view that these less conventional but more creative concerns must guide and stimulate the reform agenda. This approach has three far-reaching implications: it forces us to rethink what we mean by success and failure; it helps us formulate more imaginative, yet more realistic, proposals for change; it sheds new light on the global constituency for multilateral reform.

To grapple with this rather large and potentially unmanageable agenda, the conveners of the project made a number of strategic choices and commissioned three studies, each of which deals with an area that is important in its own right but crucially connects with the larger concerns outlined above. The central themes of these three studies (democratizing global governance; governance of global financial flows; and global peace and security) correspond to the three sections that make up the core of this publication. Given that each of the three themes itself covers a rather large area, the project has had to sharpen its focus by strategically selecting the main issues to be addressed.

In Part 1, 'Democratizing global governance', we identify the growing gap between *de facto* and *de jure* institutions of global governance as the central problem of our time. While the UN system is legally in charge of international peace and security, it is chiefly the actions of well-armed states that exacerbate or settle international conflicts. While state sovereignty is still legally the cornerstone of the international political system, it is primarily transnational actors that effectively shape global financial and economic markets. In other words, global legal institutions have not kept pace with the reach and power of political and economic actors outside the effective control of states. The study argues that if unchecked current trends will exacerbate conflicts between rich and poor within and between states, and weaken still further the social and political fabric of existing states without substituting alternative forms of legitimate governance. It concludes by offering a number of proposals for bridging this gap, with the accent on long-term structural reform.

In Part 2, 'Governance of financial flows', we begin with a brief review of the nature and impact of economic globalization, and proceed to an equally brief description of the main features of the globalization of financial/capital flows. We then survey and evaluate a number of recent proposals for regional and international regulation of financial flows, before setting out the principles that should govern sustainable social and human development at the national, regional and global level.

At the global level, the study concentrates on four key areas: making the Bretton Woods institutions accountable to a reformed UN system; developing a world financial framework; reforming the IMF; and integrating civil society concerns and agencies into the reform of the international financial system.

In Part 3, 'Global peace and security', we focus on peacekeeping, peace enforcement and humanitarian intervention, without neglecting issues of conflict transformation, and disarmament and arms control. In examining the prospects for multilateral peace operations we begin by reviewing the UN's experience in the Cold War and post-Cold War periods. We then proceed to an analysis of a number of reform proposals developed since the publication in June 1992 of Boutros Boutros-Ghali's *An Agenda for Peace*. Our approach, however, is somewhat different. We spell out the normative and organizational principles that should govern the UN's security agenda generally, and peacekeeping and peace enforcement operations in particular.

While mindful of the requirements of efficiency, timeliness of response, and clarity of mandates, we argue that the evaluation of success or failure must ultimately rest on the achievement of certain basic principles. We identify three primary principles: minimization of violence, conflict resolution, and lasting relief of unacceptable levels of human suffering; and four subsidiary principles: legitimacy, democracy, effectiveness and efficiency. To be viable, any reform agenda must pursue these principles simultaneously in the short, medium and long terms, and ensure that the various time frames are mutually consistent and reinforcing.

Notwithstanding the many obstacles that lie ahead, there is reason to suggest that the programme for reform outlined here is likely to resonate with a great many constituencies:

- those at the margins in the South but also those in the North who have borne the main costs of globalization;
- intellectual elites sensitive to the magnitude of the contemporary human predicament and to the potential of institutional innovation;
- national and international civil servants, and many in the professional classes, who understand the complexities of transnational problems and the deficiencies of existing problem-solving mechanisms;
- new voices in civil society that are increasingly skilled in articulating a new conception of international citizenship;
- a great many diplomats, generals and corporate managers who have come to see the need for more effective regulation of international transactions and more participatory decision-making structures and processes.

Though still at an embryonic stage, a loose but potent coalition for global governance reform is beginning to take shape. This project will have amply served its purpose if it facilitates, even modestly, the growth of such a coalition.

It remains for us to acknowledge the close collaboration of the three sponsoring institutions that made this project possible: the Department of Politics, La Trobe University (Melbourne), Focus on the Global South (Bangkok) and The Toda Institute for Global Peace and Policy Research (Tokyo and Honolulu). However, the project would not have seen the light of day had it not been for the generous support of a great many other organizations and individuals. Special thanks are due to the members of the Working Group, the Eminent Persons Advisory Group, Ehito Kimura for the skill and dedication with which he performed a crucial organisational role in the formative stages of this project, and Esref Aksu whose intellectual as well as administrative contribution, his meticulous attention to detail, and above all his grasp of the complexities of the project contributed so much to its successful conclusion. The project directors are particularly grateful to George Thomas for producing a masterly abridged version of the full-length study on which this report is based, Wendy Davies for her gracious and expert assistance in editing the manuscript, the Rockefeller Brothers Fund, in particular for their hospitality at the Pocantico Retreat Center, Dr Hamid Shirvani for the generous support provided by Queens College, City University of New York, and the Dag Hammarskjöld Foundation, which helped in so many different ways.

Joseph A. Camilleri
July 2000

Reimagining the future

towards democratic governance

Summary proposals

The enormous inequities, inefficiencies and dangers of the current system of global governance have made reform both necessary and inevitable. The question is: what kind of reform, at what pace, under whose initiative and with whose participation? The proposals briefly summarized here and developed at greater length in the body of the report set out possible answers to these questions. Despite the tensions and difficulties that will no doubt emerge in the process of implementation, this project rests on the conviction that to succeed any reform agenda must enshrine three distinct yet closely connected principles: human security, political democracy and socio-economic justice.

For the purposes of this study, 'short term' is used to describe a period covering anything between a few months and two years, 'medium term' anything between two and ten years, and 'long term' anything beyond ten years (generally 20-30 years).

1

Democratizing global governance

OVERARCHING PRINCIPLES

- Democratic reform of global governance means increasing democratization at all levels. It means greater participation, transparency and accountability by states and non-state actors in international decision-making, not least in the structures and processes of the United Nations.

- Ensuring balanced access to mass media and communication is vital to creating an informed public, and therefore to democratizing governance.

- Given that inequalities of wealth and income lead to unequal access to knowledge and influence, democratizing governance both requires and promotes distributive justice.

INITIATIVES

- The composition and structure of the Security Council should be changed, with the phasing out of the veto power over a fifteen to twenty year period. Initially, permanent members would retain the veto, but limitations would be placed on the frequency with which it is used. Great powers would retain permanent membership, but such membership would be reviewed, perhaps every ten years.

- To ensure greater representation, the membership of the Security Council should be expanded from 15 to 23 or 25, with permanent members expanded to seven or nine, and two rotating members (each serving a three-year term) drawn from each of eight suggested regions.

- A *People's Assembly* would be established. It would not have any legislative functions, but would operate as a house of review, carefully monitoring the decisions and deliberations of other UN bodies. Members of the People's Assembly would be directly elected (every four years) by their constituencies on the basis of universal suffrage, a secret ballot and the principle of one vote one value (with each constituency having an approximate population of 6 million, i.e. an electorate of between 3.5 and 4 million).

- A *Consultative Assembly* would also be created, with membership drawn from three main types of organization: transnational firms; trade unions and professional associations, and a range of educational, scientific, cultural, religious, and public-interest organizations (NGOs) active around the issues central to the UN's agenda.

- The General Assembly should establish a new high-level independent *Financial Advisory Committee* with the aim of substantially increasing the UN's access to financial resources, and placing it on a sounder financial footing over the next ten years.
- The UN should be authorized to issue world citizenship rights and responsibilities to qualified individual applicants.
- To enable communities and individuals to have a say in the vital decisions that affect their future, several initiatives are proposed under relevant UN auspices, including a *Global Commons Bank*, a *World Human Development Trust*, a *Women's Development Bank*, and a *World Educational Fund*.
- The UN General Assembly should immediately establish a standing *UN Reform Commission* with a distinguished but representative membership to consider the changes proposed here and elsewhere. Its first report should be completed within a year.

Governance of global financial flows

GENERAL PRINCIPLES

- Economic and financial policies should be means to sustainable human development and not an end in themselves.
- Financial and capital flows should exist to support transactions in the real economy of goods and services and not take on a life of their own, independent from the real economy.
- The principle of subsidiarity must consistently prevail.
- States and their governments must be able to exercise greater national autonomy in policy choice.
- Making national, regional and global governance mechanisms more participatory and accountable to citizens is both desirable and necessary for the achievement of sustainable human development.
- A greater role is required for the United Nations (as a relatively more democratic and representative body) in economic and social policy compared to the Bretton Woods institutions and the WTO.
- There needs to be recognition of the indivisibility of economic, social and political rights, policies and governance issues, and no artificial separation or compartmentalization of these.

INITIATIVES

- A Currency Transactions Tax on international foreign exchange transactions should be implemented nationally, within the framework of an international co-operation agreement.

- A supranational body, an *International Taxation Organization*, with participating member states as its Board of Governors and accountable to the UN, should take responsibility for the allocation of revenues.

- Capital controls at the national level, especially on inflows, should be phased out in a gradual manner, and only when and if the institutional capacity to manage such a phasing-out is firmly in place at national, regional and global levels as part of a coherent and comprehensive world financial framework.

- The creation of regional, or where appropriate, sub-regional monetary institutions or arrangements (e.g. *East Asian Monetary Fund*) is proposed. The objective would be both to have institutions that are more responsive to regional and country-specific realities and differences and to encourage greater competition and pluralism.

- Most important is the creation of a new, broadly based *Economic and Social Security Council* as a principal entity of the UN, replacing the current Economic and Social Council (ECOSOC) and accountable to the General Assembly. The Economic and Social Security Council, without veto power, should in the longer term take on key decision-making roles in its areas of mandate, similar to those of the reformed Security Council.

- A coherent, consistent and comprehensive world financial framework should be established, which encompasses institutions and arrangements at the national, regional and global levels respecting the principle of subsidiarity and based on national and regional building blocks and institutional arrangements. In the long run, this framework should be further formalized and a *World Financial Authority* should be created under UN auspices, as the overall regulator of finance at the global level. This should be accountable to the Economic and Social Security Council.

- With respect to the International Monetary Fund (IMF), the following are proposed:
  - limiting its operations to its original narrow mandate of surveillance and stabilization;
  - no change to its Charter mandate on capital account convertibility;
  - universal implementation of its surveillance role, with particular emphasis on the implementation of this role *vis-à-vis* industrialized countries.

- An *International Independent Debt Arbitration Mechanism* should be created under the broad auspices of the United Nations. Such a mechanism should address the invidious current situation where creditors are also the arbiters and unilateral judges of debt.

Global peace and security

GENERAL PRINCIPLES

- Global governance reform must make international decision-making processes more effective and efficient but also more legitimate and democratic. Placed more specifically in the context of peace and security, the reform agenda must formally adopt as key objectives, and benchmarks of success, three key principles: transparency of decision-making; extensive participation and consultation; and rigorous levels of accountability.

Disarmament and arms control

KEY PRINCIPLES

- Disarmament and arms control negotiations should over 25-30 years place clearly defined, verifiable, and carefully monitored limits on arms production and trade.
- All states possessing or producing nuclear, biological or chemical weapons should be locked into binding schedules for the freezing, reduction and elimination of their arsenals and production capabilities.

INITIATIVES

- A multi-track mobilization is needed, with a new upgraded UN Department for Disarmament and Arms Regulation (UNDDAR), the Secretary-General, and the relevant committees and working groups of the General Assembly embarking on ongoing first-track and second-track consultations on the objectives and strategies of an integrated campaign.
- A *permanent forum of all NWFZ Treaty Secretariats* should be created. Meeting at strategic times, two or three times a year, the Forum could seek to promote the consolidation and strengthening of existing zones, provide assistance to other regions contemplating zone establishment,

liaise closely with UNDDAR and other UN disarmament bodies, share information and resources on verification processes, and promote more effective lobbying and international pressure towards wider disarmament objectives and strategies.

- A comprehensive light weapons control programme should:
  - destroy all illicit weapons after they are seized;
  - incorporate mandatory and public destruction of weapons and ammunition;
  - provide international regulation of all arms exports (using codes of conduct developed and applied by regional organizations and arms control regimes but with regional practices registered with and monitored by UN);
  - mark weapons at the points of manufacture and import;
  - improve keeping of records.

Conflict transformation

KEY PRINCIPLES

- In devising a global preventive action plan, the UN must adopt a multi-track strategy, engaging and consulting with a wide range of social and political actors at all tiers of governance.

INITIATIVES

- A 'Lessons Learned' unit must be established in *all* relevant UN departments ('lessons' must draw on both successes and failures).
- A UN National Office in every member state should oversee all UN activities in that country, with conflict transformation as part of its brief (it would also facilitate other UN peace and security activities).
- Establishment of an *International Crisis Prevention and Response Centre* is proposed – supported where possible by regional crisis centres.
- There should be early establishment of an independent, well-resourced but accountable *International Criminal Court.*

Peace operations

KEY PRINCIPLES

- The UN should avoid the use or threat of force, except as a *last resort.* Its use should be strictly limited and seek to:

- prevent the outbreak of hostilities or end the violence (a high priority should be given to the prevention of genocide);
- bring quick and lasting relief to unacceptable levels of human suffering;
- promote the long-term co-existence of the conflicting parties.
- The following conditions should apply to any decision to intervene:
  - all reasonable attempts at preventive diplomacy have been tried and failed;
  - all appropriate sanctions have been applied and failed over a reasonable time-frame;
  - there is a reasonable prospect of preventing civilian casualties and of the intervention achieving its objectives in quick and enduring fashion;
  - where intervention is necessary on urgent humanitarian grounds, an *Independent Review Tribunal* will be convened to weigh up the arguments for and against intervention, and make a recommendation to the Security Council.
- The UN should retain explicit and ultimate authority over the conduct of any peace operation.

INITIATIVES

- The mandate, which gives effect to peacekeeping or peace enforcement, should set out:
  - the kind of operation that is envisaged;
  - the objectives and legal grounds for intervention;
  - the forces to be introduced;
  - the conclusion of an impact assessment conducted by an independent, adequately staffed and well-resourced *Impact Assessment Office* located in the *Department of Peace Operations* (to replace the Department of Peacekeeping Operations) and accountable to the UN Secretary-General;
  - a number of termination criteria, including the social, political, legal or military conditions which should apply for the withdrawal or scaling down of the operation.
- To strengthen its capacity for effective intervention, the UN should develop a stronger rapid reaction capability, including:
  - the creation of a permanent civilian police force;

- ○ a readily available pre-positioned stock of basic military equipment;
- ○ rosters of different types of military and civilian personnel, provided with adequate and standardized training that can be enlisted at short notice.

- Peace operations must be accompanied by an *Ombudsman*.

- An *International Peace Operations Centre* should be created that recommends to the Secretary-General international training standards, develops training materials, mounts training programmes, and keeps a detailed record of the training activities of all contributing states.

- A *Strategic Committee* should co-ordinate the political and military components of each operation, reconcile the needs of humanitarian action with the strategies and techniques of peacekeeping or peace enforcement, and more generally strike a balance between military effectiveness and political legitimacy. To this end an amendment to the UN Charter would be necessary.

- The Strategic Committee would be advised by a *Force Contributors Committee* and serviced by the *Department of Peace Operations* and a *Peace Operations Adviser* who would act as its Chief of Staff.

- The *Force Contributors Committee* would function as a standing committee comprising one representative from each of the leading contributing nations.

- The *General Staff for Peace Operations*, located within the Department of Peace Operations, would comprise a fully professional permanent military and civilian staff comprised of several units (e.g. military, police, human rights, electoral, administrative).

- An *Integrated Task Force* on the ground would liaise with UN agencies, other humanitarian organizations and representatives of the parties to the conflict.

- For each peace operation, a *Force Contributors Panel* would be established, and would comprise one representative from each contributing nation.

Part 1

Democratizing global governance

The evolution of gobal governance

Systems of large-scale international trade and co-operation can be traced back many centuries, beginning in Europe and Asia and extending to Africa and the New World. Global governance, however, with its treaties and other formal arrangements among governments, can be said to have begun in 1814 with the Congress of Vienna, which sought to stabilize Europe in the post-Napoleonic period, with a balance among the great powers.

In the years following the Congress, a system of consultation and conferences developed, which came to be known as the Concert of Europe. The Concert provided a communication channel among the European states, without infringing on their sovereignty or proposing a common moral consensus. For the 90 years that the Concert lasted, there was only one major international war, the Crimean.

In 1823, the United States enunciated the Monroe Doctrine, which formally separated the United States from the affairs of Europe, as well as declaring its opposition to any further European colonization in the Americas. European countries largely acquiesced to this declaration, which represented the first standard of conduct between Europe and the United States.

The 19th century also saw the beginnings and growth of many important international non-governmental organizations, such as the Universal Postal Union, the Red Cross and the United International Bureau for the Protection of Intellectual Property. With developments in telecommunications and transport technology facilitating trade, travel and communications, the world began to move towards becoming a single economic unit. Countries became less self-sufficient, but more interdependent and prosperous.

A system of international law gradually began to develop. Conferences at The Hague in 1899 and 1907 established the basis for a permanent court of arbitration and the conventions for the peaceful settlement of international disputes. The basis was laid for a system of global governance to regulate international affairs for the general good.

These developments took place at first only among the European countries and their past and present colonies. The ancient civilizations of Asia east of the Middle East remained apart until the technological, military and industrial power of the expansionist West became irresistible. The West thus controlled the early shaping of the forms of the global system that persist today.

World War I demonstrated many of the shortcomings of the international system; after the war, the League of Nations was formed in response. However, the League was weakened by the failure of the United States to join and by the conditions of the Treaty of Versailles, with its punitive impositions on Germany. When Hitler came to power in 1933, he withdrew Germany from the League.

Although the League achieved minor successes in the peaceful settlement of international disputes and set an important precedent for international co-operation, it was unable to prevent military aggression by Japan in Manchuria, Italy in Ethiopia, and Germany in Austria. It collapsed early in World War II.

The League succeeded in establishing the Permanent Court of Justice in 1922. It formed a Financial Commission, which reduced trade barriers and reconstructed the international monetary system, but was unable to prevent the Great Depression. It also set up the International Labour Organization: (ILO), which flourishes still. However, in its primary activities the League failed to overcome the inherent tension between ideas of national self-determination and collective security.

The Great Depression, World War II and the advent of nuclear weapons convinced the world of the necessity of institutions with more effective control over international peace, security and economic affairs. This time, importantly, the United States, now the world's most powerful country, not only joined in, but played a central role. The three Allied powers of the war (the United States, the Soviet Union and Britain) laid the foundations for the United Nations during the war, its Charter being unanimously adopted by the 50 nations that attended the San Francisco conference just before the war's end.

Problems relating to membership, colonies and voting formulas beset the United Nations from the beginning. As the five permanent members of the Security Council each had, and still have, the right to veto any resolution, and the UN Charter places the responsibility for the maintenance of international peace and security chiefly on the Council, then only with the unanimity of those five permanent members could peace and security be maintained. With the tensions of the Cold War evident from the beginning, such unanimity was certain to be rare.

The Soviet Union's frequent use of its veto in the 1950s led to the Western allies transferring the major decision-making in the UN to its General Assembly. But as colonies gained independence during the 1950s and 1960s, the newly-independent nations soon formed a numerical majority which again often led to frustration on the part of the Western allies.

Although its prime goal of world peace and security seemed remote, the UN, through its specialized agencies, was succeeding in many of its other areas of activity. The Bretton Woods institutions of the World Bank, the International Monetary Fund (IMF) and the General Agreement on Tariffs and Trade (GATT – since 1995 the World Trade Organization: WTO) respectively oversaw great advances in economic development, currency exchange and stability, and international trade. The Food and Agriculture Organization (FAO), the UN Educational, Scientific and Cultural Organization (UNESCO), the World Health Organization (WHO), the International Civil Aviation Organization (ICAO) and the World Meteorological Organization (WMO) all helped advance international co-operation and development, as did the treaties on the peaceful and co-operative exploration of outer space. So even as the UN appeared to be failing in its central purpose, its many subsidiary activities brought nations together for their mutual benefit and facilitated a significant measure of international co-operation and mutual aid.

Disaffection with an organization that in the 1970s appeared to represent principally anti-Western interests was particularly strong in the United States. The less-developed countries, despite their numerical power in the General Assembly, continued to claim that existing international systems treated them badly in comparison with the developed nations, and that the benefits of technological change went primarily to the wealthier nations. The United States, the UN's greatest source of financial support, began to lose faith with the UN and default on its dues. Moreover, armed conflict in the less-developed countries continued, the UN doing little to end or mitigate the Iran-Iraq war of the 1980s, for example, which killed or maimed about 2 million people.

The emerging international organizations were increasingly bypassing the formal UN system to achieve their aims. Some (such as the International Maritime Organization: IMO) had been set up by the UN, but most (such as Amnesty International, the World Wildlife Fund and the International Telecommunications Satellite Organization: INTELSAT) had grown to meet special needs that were best achieved outside national or UN control. Meanwhile, with the boom in telecommunications and international travel, networks of co-operation had simply grown spontaneously to meet arising demand. Satellite communications fostered new industries in which private ownership controlled many aspects of telecommunications, blurring state boundaries. Once again, however, the technology to take advantage of these advances has largely been in the hands of the wealthier citizens of the wealthier countries.

Despite the end of the Cold War and the consequent opportunities for international consensus, the UN, largely through the neglect – benign or otherwise – of the major powers, has not taken advantage of the opportunities to reform and pursue global governance. However, many of the major UN conferences of the post-Cold War period – on, for example, children's rights, climate change, population, and social development – have led to genuine progress in their respective areas.

Much of the progress in the period has been largely due to non-governmental organizations (NGOs). Recent Nobel Peace Prizes to the International Campaign to Ban Landmines, to Médecins sans Frontières, to Rigoberta Menchú of Guatemala and to Joseph Rotblat of Pugwash Conference on Science and World Affairs, have recognized this work. An organization set up in 1997, Transparency International, publishes an annual index that ranks the extent of corruption in 85 nations, thus encouraging openness and democracy. Global Action to Prevent War is another example of a significant NGO initiative. The non-partisan, voluntary nature of these organizations gives them credibility and flexibility which neither governments nor the UN can match.

The growth of global capitalism, in which international commerce transcends and to a large extent ignores national borders and government regulation, represents one of the greatest challenges to the international community. Together with the trend towards a greater role for civil society organizations (CSOs) of various types, from the beneficial to the criminal, global capitalism forms part of a complex *de facto* system of global governance. The challenge for the international community is to rationalize and democratize this complexity into a *de jure* system. In the meantime the gap between *de facto* and *de jure* grows, and the consequences of this gap can be seen in the tax evasion by transnational corporations (TNCs), the Asian financial debacle of 1997, and the growth of crony and mafia capitalism, among other serious problems.

The development of international law and institutions has not kept pace with the world's rapidly changing technological and economic environments. The gap between the global reach and power of the *de facto* and *de jure* institutions of global governance is considerable and widening.

In this report we use the term civil society organization to refer to the wide range of voluntary associations that have their own distinctive identity and sense of belonging, are independent of the state, yet help to shape community, economy and public discourse. Included in this notion are clans and villages, local communities of various kinds, groups for leisure and charity, labour unions and professional associations, scientific, intellectual, religious, cultural, and sporting organizations. CSOs are to be distinguished from NGOs, a narrower term often used to denote those associations which purport to represent the public interest. Active around such issues as development, human rights, gender, environment or peace, NGOs, particularly the larger ones, are usually committed to the development of a high-profile advocacy role. In this sense, NGOs should be seen as a distinctive subset of CSOs.

The *de facto* institutions consist of the TNCs in the economic arena and the handful of powerful states in the political arena. The *de jure* institutions comprise the intergovernmental organizations (IGOs) and the declarations and treaties on human rights and democratic principles.

Taming global capitalism

Riding the waves of accelerating scientific and technological progress, capitalism has entered a new phase of its development characterized by a transition from the confines of state territories to a global arena. This new phase may be called global capitalism. Although global capitalism has created a market of unprecedented productivity and penetration, it has failed to provide equitable or sustainable development, or to regulate itself. Transnational political, economic and cultural institutions have not yet been developed to meet the challenges of this new global civilization. The development of such institutions of global governance is the single most important challenge of the 21st century.

Global governance is not the same as global government. Whereas the world does not have a global government, it is ruled by a set of *de jure* as well as *de facto* principles and institutions that constitute global governance. These include formal declarations and treaties and international organizations, as well as the TNCs, NGOs, and crime syndicates (which are estimated to gross US$1.5 trillion a year).

Unlike previous developments in capitalism, global capitalism depends less on land or capital than on information and knowledge industries. Control of research and development, patents, licences, copyright and associated knowledge industries is critical. Since the demise of the Soviet order, global capitalism has had the entire world as its marketplace.

Global capitalism has the following characteristics:

Dynamism. It uses science and technology to create constant change.

Optimism. It promises that those who embrace its precepts will be better off.

Globalism. It reaches all over the world, helped in recent years by the trend towards free trade and deregulation of economies.

Information technology. Introduction of computer-assisted design, manufacturing, inventory, just-in-time production and sales (electronic commerce), and the free and instantaneous exchange of information and money anywhere in the world.

Informatic imperialism. Freed by technology from local constraints, global capitalism can move to wherever levels of wages, rents, taxes, and government regulation and support can guarantee the highest profits.

Flexible capital accumulation. Production need not be centralized, but can be dispersed in the production of parts and assembly of the final product in various areas of the world.

Transnational corporations. Most of the largest 100 economic units in the world are not nations, but TNCs which, with their size and mobility, have immense bargaining power, including the power to influence, and even overthrow, governments. Their strength stems from centralized, strategic and global decision-making, combined with decentralized operations in many parts of the world.

Institutional support. The Bretton Woods institutions have facilitated, and continue to support, the growth of global capitalism, with their advocacy of free trade and deregulation and their punishment of those nations that do not toe the line.

Competition with states and societies. Global capitalism has diminished the power of states and can often afford to ignore any harmful local effects from its activities. Civil society, particularly in the form of NGOs, has been revived in response.

Ambivalence towards democracy. Although stable democratic institutions provide the best operating environment, global capitalism has been prepared to support stability at the expense of freedom and justice.

Oligopoly. While most industries are more or less dominated by a few TNCs, some industries (such as computers, aerospace, the media and pharmaceuticals) are almost entirely controlled by them.

Destabilization. Unregulated capitalism creates cycles of boom and bust, and an unequal distribution of wealth and power, all of which tends to cause social and political instability. Global capitalism's mobility also causes local booms in currently favoured locations, then busts when that location loses favour.

Environmental damage. Often the most profitable locations are those with the least environmental regulation. With little need to commit itself to a locality, global capitalism has caused great environmental damage in less-regulated areas.

Commodity and identity fetishism. Those who embrace global capitalism tend to engage in conspicuous consumption, while those who miss out tend to fall back on cultural, religious or racial identities as a defence.

Inequity. The rise of global capitalism has been followed by a rise in inequality between richer and poorer nations and between the rich and the poor within nations.

The poor nations under global capitalism are the same nations that were poor under colonialism. Under the new colonialism, the low-tech and high-polluting industries are located in the less-developed nations, while high-tech and knowledge industries stay in the richer countries. Meanwhile, the manual workers from the richer nations watch their jobs disappear to the less-developed nations.

One feature of global capitalism is a two-tiered mass population movement. At the top of the social structure are the global elite, roaming the world as managers, guardians and celebrants of the global economy. At the bottom are the refugees and the millions seeking escape from squalor and misery, either by crossing national borders or by migrating from the country to the cities. The global elite and the global underclass are colliding in the major metropolitan centres: the elite in the luxury hotels and houses, the underclass in the slums.

What amounts to a global apartheid does not provide a stable system for its inhabitants. Requiring free flows of goods, services, capital, labour, ideas and information across state boundaries, and characterized by porous borders and ethnic divisions, the global economy is vulnerable to recession, protectionism, sabotage and terrorism.

On the positive side of global capitalism are its relentless technological innovation, economic growth and affluence. On the negative side – in addition to the problems of inequality – the problems of pollution, epidemic diseases, wars, drug trafficking, money laundering, arms-dealing and financial corruption all increasingly tend to ignore national borders. The future of global capitalism depends on whether or not it can solve the problems of inequality and dislocation generated by its spectacular economic and technological success.

Holding the peace

At the end of history's bloodiest century, the international community faces the challenge of resolving tensions and using the creative elements in prevailing trends to achieve co-operation instead of conflict. That challenge will involve the democratization of global governance in a way that can best accommodate the interests and perspectives of the world's inhabitants.

Modernity, especially as it is propagated by the forces of global capitalism, creates insecurities as it privileges the new and the young against the old, the nascent against the declining, the strong against the weak. It thus marginalizes vast segments of the population and leads to conflicts of cultures, values and identities that cannot easily be resolved. Recent armed conflicts in many places (such as Chechnya, Kosovo and Tajikistan) cannot be understood unless they are viewed against the larger picture of global capitalism. Usually those who are in revolt against global capitalism seek not to resist modernity as such, but to take control of development away from global forces and put it into local and national hands.

The moral geographies of the new order have shifted from the bipolar rivalries of the Cold War towards a contestation among different forces and interests. Seven major trends are currently influencing international affairs: *globalism, regionalism, nationalism, localism, environmentalism, feminism* and *religious revivalism*. Each trend suggests a potential power shift that may lead to fundamental changes in the world. Each trend has its inherent tensions, which could lead to co-operative security or to competitive insecurity.

The practice and health of democracy is perhaps the key factor in directing these trends towards peaceful outcomes. But democracy thrives best in the smallest and most intimate aggregations of communities, notably in neighbourhoods, villages and towns. The level of distortion in communication and representation increases as the distance between the elector and the elected grows. There are no guarantees for democracy unless each trend moves away from hegemony and exclusion and towards communitarian and inclusive systems of power and participation.

Globalism

For several centuries, capitalism has been the engine of globalism, sweeping aside old loyalties and traditions in favour of the internationalization of the world. The chief technologies of economic expansion have been those of energy, transportation and telecommunication. Without telecommunication, trans-border data flows and electronic fund transfers, the global economy and the TNC could not exist.

Global capitalism has produced spectacular successes and disastrous failures. It has brought modern industrial civilization to the remotest regions of the world, but it has also created huge gaps and antagonisms between rich and poor, humans and nature, dominant and repressed ethnicities, and centres and peripheries. Whereas poverty in traditional societies is made tolerable by relative equality, the ethics of self-denial and mutual obligation, and the bonds of community, modernized poverty is characterized by rootless and atomistic mobility, social envy, frustration, regression and aggression. And the contradictions of the modern world (such as time-consuming acceleration, stupefying education and information-void news) frequently offset the gains.

Globalism is torn between hegemonic and counter-hegemonic trends. In the debate on how best to shape the world order in the post-Cold War era, five schools of thought have emerged: neo-isolationism, unilateralism, trilateralism, multilateralism, and communitarian globalism.

Neo-isolationism. The impact of free trade on low-paid jobs in developed countries has led to calls, especially in the United States, for a reinstitution of protectionism and a reliance on national self-sufficiency rather than trade for prosperity. In many nations there have also been reactions against immigration from the Third World.

Unilateralism. According to this viewpoint, the United States, as the only superpower, must act as the defender of Western interests and values.

Trilateralism. Trilateralists see the three major economic entities of the United States, Western Europe and Japan as collective world leaders.

Multilateralism. Through the United Nations and its agencies, and stimulated by the unanimity of the five permanent members of the Security Council, multilateralism has its supporters and has had some practical success.

Communitarian globalism, or globalism from below, is another powerful force, assisted by global communication networks and an emerging international civil society organized around the multitude of CSOs.

Regionalism

Given the heterogeneity of the world, global community is perhaps best achieved through an interlocking system of smaller and more homogeneous communities. The world may have already entered the age of regions, if the progress of NAFTA, the EU and ASEAN is an indication. The danger is that the regions will become chauvinistic and antagonistic to each other, rather than outward-looking and seeking to represent their respective interests to, and co-operate with, the rest of the world.

As regional groupings prove their worth to their respective members, more countries in other regions are likely to seek the benefits of membership of such bodies, and to enhance those more rudimentary groupings that already exist. However, regional integration requires economic complementarity, political stability and trust, which even in the more successful groupings are hard to maintain, and in most countries are rare to begin with.

Nationalism

Because it is closer to the realities of human diversity than is regionalism, nationalism has proved relatively successful in the modern world. It has gone through three distinct phases. In the century to the end of World War I, nationalism united the principalities of Europe into a series of relatively homogeneous nation-states. Between the wars the idea of self-determination stirred the liberation movements of the colonised world, which after World War II led to the fall of colonialism and the rise of the newly-independent states. Since the end of the Cold War, ethno-nationalism has risen to challenge prevailing national entities on behalf of previously suppressed cultural minorities. Many of the violent conflicts around the world today are ethnic wars.

Nationalism can be a positive force for unifying, strengthening or liberating a people. It can also lead to the most malignant expressions of ethnic hatred.

The three main schools of thought in the debate on nationalism are the primordialists, the instrumentalists and the communitarians.

Primordialism. According to this line of thinking, national identity is based on some deep collective unconscious embedded in the language and beliefs of a national group.

Instrumentalism. Instrumentalists try to show how nationalism is used as a means to achieve a particular goal.

Communitarianism. Here the argument is that national identity is constructed from historical memories and is constantly adjusting itself to changed circumstances.

History is replete with examples of policies that have attempted to mould the national identity to suit the state. Such policies have included extermination (e.g. the Jews in Nazi Germany), segregation (e.g. apartheid), assimilation (the dominant policy in most Western countries since World War II), amalgamation (where dual allegiance, to the nation and to one's ethnic group, is accepted) and pluralism (where differences are celebrated).

Localism

Localism is a reaction against both centralized government and globalism. It seeks, wherever possible, to give decision-making power to the people who are affected by the decisions. It values local knowledge and custom above state power or the collective wisdom of the nation, and emphasizes participation above politics.

Like nationalism, localism can be a positive force, returning a measure of participatory democracy to the people and expressing the aspirations of communities, or it can be parochial and exclusive, a vehicle for the expression of fear and hatred. A community can aggravate existing inequity by using localism to defend its privileges instead of using its privileged position to assist its less fortunate neighbours. Unless such inequities are tackled, they can cause irreparable damage to global, national, or local sense of community of common destiny.

Environmentalism

Because of the growing strength and breadth of the movement towards environmental awareness, development in the more advanced countries has in recent decades come to take into account its effects on the environment, and environmental degradation that had seemed only to be getting worse has been slowed, stopped or even reversed in some cases. However, while the more developed countries have begun to deal with environmental problems – admittedly this is a rather small beginning – the less developed countries face an urgent need for rapid development and tend consequently to neglect environmental protection. Some of the problem stems from TNCs moving their pollution-creating industries to the developing countries.

The movement for sustainable development is now worldwide and broad-based. Linked with its concern about destruction of the environment is concern about the destruction of communities, and the realization that our bonds with nature and with our communities are too valuable to be sold for short-term profit in the drive to modernize.

The need for a new balance between liberty, equality and community is central to the communitarian perspective. The communitarian seeks to bring to national and international levels the values essential to the health of a local community: common interests, norms, laws and sanctions. We have a common interest in seeking to avert the threats of ecological disasters and wars; an emerging consensus on international norms recognizes global interdependence; and for norms to have effect there must be laws, and sanctions to uphold those laws.

Feminism

One of history's greatest revolutionary changes is the ongoing struggle of women for freedom and equality. Despite the progress that has been made worldwide, there is still much to be done to counter and eradicate discrimination against women in both advanced and developing nations. Since feminism appears to many men as part of a global trend threatening their way of life, reactions against the equality of women often form part of general reactions against universalizing human rights.

Revivalism

The secular ideologies of progress (nationalism, liberalism, communism) were thought for a while to be providing a new enlightened sense of community and responsibility, and sweeping aside the old religious, racial and ethnic identities. But they never resolved the human conditions of finitude, fragility and moral frailty. Ethnic or national culture as a defence against the alienating onslaught of globalism has thus assumed new vitality.

The modern world, despite its successes, has failed to provide fairness or a sense of community, or to take account of the moral and spiritual needs of individuals or society. A new religious revivalist spirit, present in one form or another throughout the world, has sought to remedy this shortfall. The movement has two faces: sectarian and ecumenical. In countries as different as the United States, India, Egypt, Indonesia and Israel, politics is strongly influenced by religious movements, usually in opposition to what they see as the harmful trends of modernity.

Religious movements, particularly when their stance is relatively moderate, may enter the mainstream of the cultural and political life of a country. Other strategies include revolutionary militancy (in an attempt to seize power themselves), withdrawal from mainstream society, accommodation with the rest of society, or a determined conserving of traditional values.

In some cases a religious movement may moderate its claims to total truth and develop a tolerance towards other beliefs. Or it may become rigid and defiant, causing division and conflict in society.

Threats to peace

The various global threats to security – war, ecological disaster, social disintegration – are leading to the emergence of a new sense of oneness in the world, the understanding that we exist interdependently. This realization draws on the heritage of the wisdom of all the world's religions and philosophies.

At the same time the threats to peace continue to abound. The tension that has been characterized as 'Jihad versus McWorld' – identity fetishism versus commodity fetishism – shows signs only of worsening, as globalization intensifies and pushes local identities aside with its undeliverable promises of wealth and ease for all.

But glib, catchy terms obscure the complexity of the struggles, which are not simply religious and commercial, but include important ethnic, class, racial, tribal, moral, social, political and other aspects. Unless these complexities are taken into account in the search for solutions to the problems that threaten to engulf us all, new cycles of violence are assured, from which none of us is likely to find refuge.

Democratizing governance

The enormous inequities, inefficiencies and dangers of the current system of *de facto* global governance make the shift to a system of *de jure* global governance essential. No such reform can take place without the consensus of the major states. A period of intense and wide-ranging discussion, with participation from the broadest possible range of governments, organizations and the public is therefore necessary. The aim is simple: a far greater level of global democracy than currently prevails. The achievement of this aim is likely to involve a complex and difficult process. The proposals at the end of this section and in subsequent sections outline a possible design for this process.

Modern democracy has evolved in at least four waves. The first wave began with the series of democratic revolutions in Britain, the United States and France in the 17th and 18th centuries and spread through Europe in the 19th century. The second wave was led by the working-class movements, beginning in the late 19th century and leading to social welfare and labour reforms in the industrialized countries and communist revolutions in Russia, China and other less-industrialized countries. The third wave was the anti-colonial movement, which led to the independence of the world's colonies. The fourth wave has gained momentum since the end of the Cold War, as suppressed minorities throughout the world try to assert their rights to self-determination.

A fifth democratic wave may have begun. The Asian economic crisis of 1997-98 showed how far the institutions of global governance are lagging behind the growth of TNCs in controlling world markets. A similar lag has been demonstrated in such areas as genocide, environmental degradation and weapons proliferation. The need for global governance buttressed by global democratic institutions is increasingly felt everywhere.

The territorial state is now too small for the big problems and too big for the small problems. Global democracy has to move in two directions simultaneously – to strengthen democratic participation at local levels and to broaden and formalize it at the international level. However, there are many ideological schools, each attempting to pull in its own direction. The diagram on the page opposite shows how the left-right spectrum that could accommodate most ideological schools during the Cold War has broken up into a far more complex set of rival ideologies. These can be divided into four groups, each of which can be characterized by its motivating principle: freedom, equality, community, or order. The challenge is to optimize these competing principles and to keep a balance among them rather than maximize one at the expense of the others.

The stakeholders in the structure and processes of global governance may be identified as the eternal triangle of the state, the market and civil society. The state occupies a central and powerful place, but the market – in the form of TNCs – rivals and sometimes surpasses the power of the state. Civil society, represented by a great many associations, including NGOs, does not have a comparable, readily usable power but, when mobilized, can still check and balance the activities of the other two. Other major players include the mass media – usually aligned with the market but still dependent on mass public support and various forms of government licensing and regulation – and the extra-legal organizations, from governments-in-exile to the international drug cartels.

Global policies are formed as a result of the activities and interactions of all these players, but the final shapers of policy are the major states, the intergovernmental organizations, and the transnational industrial and financial corporations. Sometimes these four groups act together, sometimes they negotiate their differences; at other times they are influenced by the lobbying of mass movements such as the coalition that successfully pushed for an international treaty on landmines. Policy is disseminated and critiqued through the mass media, the specialist media, the internet, and informal networks of communication.

A democratic drift?

The modern capitalist state that has emerged since the Cold War in the age of global capitalism is committed to three functions: military security, economic growth, and corporate and social welfare. It is an activist state, co-ordinating its functions with global capital to adjust to the changing technological and economic environment. While it is shifting some of its previous burdens to the private sector, it shows no sign of shrinking – government spending as a proportion of GDP has not fallen, and may even be continuing to rise.

Re-mapping the Global Spectrum

The Greens ☆
(1) communitarian capitalism
(2) socialism
(3) community
(4) intelligentsia
(5) superego
(6) communalism
(7) high integration
(8) tribalization
(9) identity fetishism

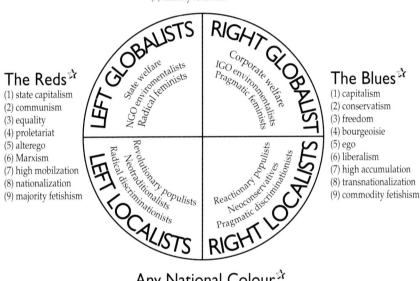

The Reds ☆
(1) state capitalism
(2) communism
(3) equality
(4) proletariat
(5) alterego
(6) Marxism
(7) high mobilzation
(8) nationalization
(9) majority fetishism

The Blues ☆
(1) capitalism
(2) conservatism
(3) freedom
(4) bourgeoisie
(5) ego
(6) liberalism
(7) high accumulation
(8) transnationalization
(9) commodity fetishism

Any National Colour ☆
(1) totalitarian capitalism
(2) nazism, fascism, militarism
(3) order
(4) big and petit bourgeoise
(5) id
(6) fascism
(7) high repression
(8) totalization
(9) security fetishism

☆ Symbolic Colour

(1) indicates social system
(2) indicates political party alignment
(3) indicates axial principle
(4) indicates leadership
(5) indicates psychic energy

(6) indicates ideology
(7) indicates development strategy
(8) indicates process
(9) indicates pathology

Adapted from Tehranian, *Worlds Apart: Human Security and Global Governance, 1999*

The modern global corporation is not tied to a particular country. It can move its operations to wherever the conditions are most propitious, and with its immense financial power it is thus able to bargain with governments from a position of strength. States now have to compete for the favour of corporations rather than, as previously, the other way around.

At the national level, the development of democratic institutions of accountability has served as a major check against unbridled capitalism. A civil society of voluntary organizations – cultural, religious, labour, sporting, political – is the backbone of all modern democratic polities. Without mass popular participation in civil society, a democratic system lacks legitimacy, and special-interest groups will often claim to represent the public interest.

At a global level, the rise of international non-governmental organizations may be about to form an analogous system of grassroots democratic participation, providing the sort of community in which global democracy can grow and flourish. Like their counterparts at national and local levels, these organizations nurture, discuss and communicate alternative points of view, and criticize and challenge official points of view. They also encourage activity outside official channels, often against or beyond officially organized and condoned activity.

Global communication is essential to all actors on the global stage. Although it has traditionally favoured those with the financial power to exploit it, especially in the mass media, the technology of global communication has also empowered democratic movements as it has become harder for governments to control how their citizens inform themselves, each other and the outside world. However, unless a country has a balance of commercial, state, public and community media, the democratic potential of modern communications – and of that country – will not be realized. The existence of a strong civil society to counter the powers of the state and the market is a precondition for media pluralism, and this applies as much to the globe as to a nation.

Conclusion and proposals

Three different scenarios may be envisaged for the future of the world: continuity, collapse and transformation.

In the continuity scenario, current trends continue. With typical capitalist busts and booms, growth will continue unevenly across the globe. Although East Asia has been the fastest-growing region in recent years, its economies may mature to the point where they no longer provide relatively low wages, rents, taxes and regulation. The TNCs may leave for Latin America or Africa. The basic structures of capitalism would not change. Liberal democracy would continue to be the predominant form of government, and the more repressive governments would have to democratize as their working class demand higher wages and their middle class insist on civil liberties.

In the collapse scenario, growing inequities among and within countries produce greater tensions and conflicts, involving more of the world's countries in large or small armed clashes, from local crime and terrorism to full-scale war.

In the transformation scenario, education and intervention prevent disaster. Such intervention may take the form of an attempt to establish world government, or it may take the opposite form, an attempt to do away with government. Alternatively, it may take more reformist and incremental forms, moving towards the establishment of the rule of law, or concentrating on building interlocking communities of interest from the local to the global.

The main hope for democratizing global governance towards greater peace and security lies in a partnership between government, business, the media and civil society. The current world order is heavily unbalanced, favouring the most powerful states and the TNCs. Both of these will have to relinquish some of their power to bring about a more just world order. The establishment of democratic checks and balances through a form of global democracy is a *sine qua non* of world survival.

In setting out a programme of democratic reform we begin with a statement of general principles derived from the preceding analysis. Here it is worth stressing that, despite tensions likely to emerge from time to time in the implementation of reform, human security, political democracy and socio-economic justice must be treated as three distinct but inextricably entwined elements of the reform agenda.

OVERARCHING PRINCIPLES

- Globalization is encroaching on the world environment, global commons, and national sovereignty in ways that are beyond the control of territorial states. Global warming, proliferation of weapons of mass destruction, tax evasion through offshore banking, and drug and arms trafficking provide examples of problems that can be solved only through international co-operation. To this extent, at least, there is an urgent need for global regulatory institutions transcending national boundaries.

- Global governance should be considered not as global government but, rather, the complex of interlocking, intergovernmental regimes and institutions that regulate the world at the local, national, regional and global levels.

- Democratic reform of global governance means democratization at all levels, including increasing transparency, accountability, and participation by the stakeholders (state and non-state actors) in the decision-making processes.

- Democratizing governance also means active participation by the trinity of governments, corporations and civil society organizations (or, more abstractly, states, markets and civil society) in decisions that affect public life at the local, national, regional and global levels.

- Since the free and balanced flow of information (news and views) is vital to informed public opinion and to the formation and expression of the democratic will, reform of the present unbalanced access to mass media – and communication, generally – lies at the heart of democratizing governance.

- Democratization of knowledge has been, historically, a driving force in democratic developments. Barriers to knowledge of whatever kind must therefore be considered as barriers to democratization. Unequal access to educational opportunities and monopoly control of scientific and technological innovations are currently the most important obstacles to democratization.

- Given that inequalities in income and wealth have led to inequalities in access to knowledge, information and power, democratizing governance must be seen as requiring and delivering distributive justice.

- Since the new interactive technologies of communication (notably the Internet) have a long-term democratic potential, they should be made universally available for public education and participation in both representative institutions and direct, democratic institutions. Reforms to the way in which election campaigns are financed must therefore include fair and equal media access for all voices.

INITIATIVES

Several intractable problems have hampered the UN's capacity to act and weakened the legitimacy of its actions. The need for greater legitimacy, which in part depends on much higher levels of participation and openness in decision-making, suggests the need for radical reform. The three aims must be: to make the Security Council a more representative institution; to enhance the effectiveness and authoritativeness of the General Assembly; and to open up the UN system to the voices of civil society, that is to a range of non-state actors and to world public opinion generally.

Security Council. To enhance its legitimacy, the Security Council must be opened up to broader membership and wider input into its discussions and decision-making processes. The veto rights of the five permanent members must be qualified and gradually phased out, over perhaps fifteen to twenty years. Initially, permanent members might retain the veto, but limitations could be placed on the frequency with which it is used or the manner in which it is exercised.

Great powers would retain permanent membership, but such membership would be reviewed, perhaps every ten years, to ensure it reflects global power realities.

To ensure greater representation, the membership of the Security Council should be expanded from the current 15 to 23 or 25. Permanent members could be expanded from five to seven or nine – at this point Germany, Japan, India and, perhaps, Brazil might be suitable candidates for permanent membership. Depending on the progress of European integration, it may be appropriate at the end of the first ten-year period for Germany, France and Britain to relinquish their permanent membership in favour of the European Union.

The Security Council's membership could be expanded along regional lines. The world could be divided into regions, one possible classification being: Western Europe, Eastern Europe and Russia, Africa, the Middle East and West and Central Asia, South Asia, East Asia and Oceania, North and Central America, and South America. Each of these eight regions could elect two representatives to the Council, each member serving a three-year term.

To pave the way for this long-term change in the composition of the Security Council, a short- to medium-term solution not requiring Charter amendment might be to give a number of states (major regional powers such as Germany, Japan, Brazil, India, Indonesia) 'semi-permanent' status. These members would be elected more frequently than other rotating members, which might also help to familiarize them with the processes and responsibilities associated with Security Council membership.

General Assembly. At its annual meeting the General Assembly should debate the reports of the Security Council and the proposed Economic and Social Security Council (see Part 2). The Assembly would then formulate guidelines for global security and economic policy in the coming year, which would provide the broad direction for the actions and deliberations of the two Councils.

Where the General Assembly deems that either Council has not acted in the spirit of those guidelines, it would have the power to request the Council to reconvene and review its decisions in the light of the advice given by the Assembly. Although the Assembly would not have the power to override the two Councils, the proposed strengthening of its authority would enable all members states to have greater input into security and economic policy-making at the global level and, at the same time, to make such policy more open to international scrutiny and debate.

People's Assembly. The Security Council and the General Assembly can only represent the governments of member states, many of which have tenuous or poor democratic credentials and questionable legitimacy. There is, therefore, a strong case for a second chamber, a People's Assembly, which would provide a forum for a much wider range of views. The People's Assembly would not have legislative powers, but would function as a house of debate and review overall aspects of UN activity.

Members would be elected by their constituencies by universal suffrage, a secret ballot, one vote one value. The boundaries of each constituency (with an approximate population of about 6 million, i.e. an electorate of between 3.5 and 4 million) would be determined by a UN electoral commission. The elections would be preceded by widespread public debate and widely accessible media coverage, and organized by the relevant national government, but closely monitored by a UN inspection team to ensure proper procedure. Each country's membership of the General Assembly would be conditional on meeting these electoral requirements. These arrangements would have a democratizing effect on the political processes of many countries including liberal democracies, improve the international image of the United Nations and encourage a better informed world public opinion.

Consultative Assembly. The overarching goal of the United Nations is to improve global conditions conducive to human security. To put it differently, the environment, population movements, food and energy security, marine resources, trade and financial flows, human rights, transnational crime and much else are integral elements of the global governance agenda. It makes good sense therefore that organizations that have a close involvement with or acknowledged expertise in these matters should have a part in the UN's debating and decision-making processes.

A third chamber, the Consultative Assembly, would consist of representatives drawn from three sectors: the corporate sector (represented through international and regional umbrella organizations); the trade union and professional sector (also through their umbrella organizations), and the 'third sector' including a wide range of educational, scientific, cultural, religious and public-interest organizations (NGOs) involved in issues of human security. The General Assembly would determine the membership of the Consultative Assembly on the recommendation of the UN Secretariat.

Secretary-General and Secretariat. The success of any reform programme will, to a considerable degree, depend on the stature, authority, and administrative and financial resources of the Secretary-General and his/her staff.

The role of the Secretary-General must be defined more clearly. First, the Secretary-General, while acting in accordance with the decisions of the UN's principal deliberative organs, must be empowered to use greater initiative, particularly when dealing with crises. In addition to preparing detailed reports for the consideration of the three Assemblies and the two Councils, the Secretary-General should also be able to submit detailed proposals and recommendations to them on a regular basis.

Second, the independence of the office being paramount, the Secretariat must be protected from any appearance of bias. The process of appointment must be transparent and the result of a much more inclusive consultative process than at present.

Third, part of the Secretary-General's role must be to articulate a vision for the UN system that is faithful to its principles and at the same time sensitive to changing world conditions.

Fourth, the Secretary-General must engage systematically with all key players in world affairs – paying particular attention to the voices of civil society.

Fifth, the Secretary-General, with the assistance of the various departments under his/her authority, must more effectively co-ordinate all the organs and activities that comprise the UN system. For this purpose, an inter-departmental/inter-agency committee should be set up – with the Secretary-General as its Chairperson, and with overall responsibility for its agenda – which would function as a Cabinet for the entire UN system.

UN Reform Commission. To consider the changes proposed here and elsewhere, the UN General Assembly should immediately establish a standing UN Reform Commission composed of distinguished representatives from the government, business, and civil society sectors to study and report on the matter. Its first report should be completed within a year.

Financial arrangements. The General Assembly should establish a new high-level independent *Financial Advisory Committee*. Its aim would be to provide the UN, over the next ten years, with greater and more reliable access to financial resources, in ways that do not compromise but rather enhance its independence. The Committee should re-examine several proposals/initiatives that have been advanced in recent years (e.g. a Peacekeeping Reserve Fund and a Revolving Credit Fund). Particular attention should be given to the introduction of an international tax – to be applied, for example, to financial transactions, air travel or arms transfers.

As a broad objective, the total amount derived from national assessments for the UN's general budget and for its peace operations budget should be increased by an annual 10 per cent over the next ten years. Over the same ten-year period, a new structure of assessments should be arrived at, such that no member state contributes more than 10 per cent to the total amount, provided that no additional burden is placed on developing economies. Any reduction in the contribution of the United States should be made up by other OECD countries and the more affluent among countries with newly industrialized economies.

If a member state fails to pay its dues on time for reasons other than acute financial hardship, penalties should be imposed (including fines and possible forfeiture of some of its voting rights). It should forfeit all its voting rights if it continues to default for two or more years in succession. Financial contributions from non-government sources should be accepted, but only under strict conditions of transparency and accountability to the General Assembly.

World citizenship. The United Nations should be authorized to issue world citizenship rights and responsibilities to qualified individual applicants who, by virtue of their intellectual, artistic, professional, administrative or other achievements, have demonstrated outstanding commitment to the UN Charter and the Universal Declaration of Human Rights. Such citizenship will be conferred upon applicants in addition to their national citizenship. It will entail certain rights and obligations that shall be defined by special international laws and statues. Those who have served in UN peace operations would also be eligible to apply. Using need as the other criterion, world citizenship rights could be extended to stateless persons and long-term refugees.

Linking democracy and socio-economic justice. The right of communities and individuals everywhere to have a say in the vital decisions that affect their future is inextricably linked to the purposes that such participation is meant to serve. We have already subsumed these under the general umbrella of human security. What follows is a series of proposed initiatives specifically designed to promote political democracy and socio-economic justice as mutually reinforcing objectives and processes. Many of these initiatives could be readily subsumed under existing UN agencies or programmes, but the intention here is to ensure that they operate with sufficient autonomy to ensure their compliance with rigorous standards of transparency, participation and accountability.

- *Global Commons Bank.* This Bank would be established under the United Nations with the dual objectives of encouraging and diffusing scientific, technological, and artistic innovations beneficial to humanity, and protecting the natural environment for the use of present and future generations. The Bank could be divided into two main subsidiaries: a *Global Knowledge Bank* and a *Global Ecology Bank.* It would be funded by private and public donations as well as a 'pollution tax' and an 'intellectual property royalty' to be levied on businesses that pollute or hold intellectual property rights beyond a pre-determined time, say five or ten years. In due course, interest payments on the Bank's loans would provide additional sources of revenues.

  The establishment of a Global Knowledge Bank would be tied to a new international intellectual property regime to regulate future copyright and patent systems. The Bank, in close collaboration with UNESCO and other appropriate international organisations, would monitor the development of global information infrastructures and provide low-interest loans to the less-developed economies to assist the growth of their telecommunication and educational institutions.

- *World Human Development Trust.* Operating under the auspices and general oversight of the UN Development Programme (UNDP), the Trust would be dedicated to eradicating poverty by focusing on investments in the provision of prenatal care, adequate child nutrition, self-help housing, public health, and public education. To finance the Trust, a global tax would be levied on all arms transfers. In order to raise the living standards of the poorest segments of world population, the Trust should be managed on the same principles as those of the micro-financing banks such as the Grameen Bank in Bangladesh.

- *Women's Development Bank.* To be established under the auspices of the UN Development Fund for Women (UNIFEM), the bank would provide loans at low interest rates, or free of interest, to low-income women. Models to be considered might include the Grameen Bank or the Self-Employed Women's Association in India. This special bank could be financed by donations, public-spirited private investments and government contributions.

- *World Educational Fund.* Operating under the auspices of UNESCO, the Fund would provide free or low-interest loans to non-profit educational institutions for upgrading their facilities or awarding scholarships to deserving individuals. The Fund would be required by its Charter to promote equal educational opportunities to all, regardless of race, colour or creed. The Fund could be financed by private and public donations, surcharges on the tuition fees charged by rich private educational institutions, and a levy applied on corporate training budgets.

Part 2

Governance of global financial flows

The context

The current dominant patterns of finance- and economics-led globalization began to take shape in the early 1970s after the collapse of the gold standard and Bretton Woods system. Many economists and politicians in the Western world pushed for greater freedom for capital movements and the deregulation of markets for capital, goods and labour. They advocated supply-side economic strategies and conservative macro-economic fiscal and monetary policies based on the reduction of inflation, even at the risk of higher unemployment. These policies became dominant in the 1980s and 1990s. There has been broad-based and intense criticism of many of these polices and some discussion about their merits as a result of the controversies surrounding the IMF's prescription of them in response to the Asian-led global financial and economic crisis that became visible and explicit in Thailand in July 1997. However, the same policies remain predominant at both the national and global levels as we enter the new millennium.

The two most important differences between current processes of globalization that have developed since the 1970s and earlier systems of economic internationalization (predominantly through trade) are the key role of the new information and communication technologies and the presence of unfettered and virtually unhampered markets as a result of explicit economic and financial liberalization policy choices that have been made in the last quarter-century.

Other differences include the ideological and selective use of free-trade theory by the advocates of economic globalization, the contrast between the mobility of capital and the relative immobility of unskilled labour, and the diminished role of the nation-state. The disproportionate growth of capital flows compared to trade in goods and services is another new development. For example, total annual currency trades are now over

US$400 trillion, which is more than ten times the world's output of goods and services! Much, if not the overwhelming majority, of such flows are speculative, for purposes of tax evasion or money-laundering without contribution to the real national or global economy of the production of goods and services.

One effect of these trends has been a kind of economic re-colonization whereby the newly-independent states of the 20th century (nearly all developing countries), still trying to develop healthy and stable economies, have lost what little control they had over their relationship with the global market in the 1950s and 1960s. Even in industrialized countries, it has become harder for governments to use economic policy to deal with unemployment or other social and environmental problems.

Current patterns of globalization have also led to serious tensions between the global and the local. In failing to share its benefits equally among all those affected by the process, globalization has engendered escalating inequalities of unprecedented proportions. Large sections of the world's population (in most of sub-Saharan Africa, for example) have benefited little, while others even in 'miracle economic growth' regions have benefited for a time, then regressed (as in significant parts of Indonesia and Thailand in the aftermath of the Asian-led global financial crisis). A major unresolved dilemma as a result is that while local actors often feel powerless to influence the forces of globalization, attempts to cut themselves off from the outside world could lead to even further marginalization rather than added protection. Even relatively powerful countries can appear impotent in this new global context.

Another worrying phenomenon of this new world disorder is that TNCs, largely based in industrialized countries and relatively unaccountable both socially and politically, have multiplied in this new environment of economic liberalization, becoming even more powerful than all but the biggest developing economies. As a result, in 1996 there were about 44,000 TNCs, of which just 500 controlled approximately 70 per cent of global trade. Of the world's 100 largest economies, more than half are now TNCs. Collectively, they can threaten the viability of a national economy if the government does not give them the operating incentives they lobby for, as in most cases they can simply relocate to a more amenable country.

Those who benefit from globalization are generally those with considerable amounts of accumulated capital or certain professional skills. Those with neither are increasingly marginalized or socially excluded. This is true both for people within countries and for countries themselves. Poorer, less-educated countries have an increasingly negligible role in the globalizing world.

Yet, it would be wrong to assume that the state as an entity is in terminal decline. In the face of global forces insensitive to local needs, the state retains a crucial role in matters concerning the public good. Until now, many governments have merely acted as facilitators for TNCs and their preferred form of globalization, assuming or hoping that their countries would benefit. In the aftermath of the Asian led crisis, however, there is some cause for optimism that they are beginning to understand that the public good rarely coincides with the private interests of TNCs.

Global financial flows

The rush, during recent decades, of capital-account liberalization has facilitated and increased the flow of capital across national borders, and international finance has begun to replace the production of goods and services as the prime mover of the world economy. Up to 2 trillion US dollars is believed to be transferred around the world every day. The flow to developing countries – mostly in the form of speculative investment unrelated to, or unnecessary for, the real economy of goods and services – has increased dramatically, leading to spectacular cycles of boom and bust, as in Mexico and East Asia during the 1990s. This trend was best exemplified by the fact that hedge funds, whose main business is speculation, increased tenfold in number and assets between 1992 and 1997; their sudden interest in, or withdrawal from, a country, especially as they are most drawn to emerging market economies where the highest short-term profits can be made, can cause disaster in the local economy.

Financial liberalization has been the key to this rise in financial flows. The 1997 *World Investment Report* indicates that of the 599 changes to regulatory regimes made by national governments between 1991 and 1996, 95 per cent were in the direction of liberalization. For those countries in trouble, there is a disincentive to reverse this liberalization, as the IMF makes its assistance conditional on a continuation of this liberalization trend. Those developing countries that depend most on trade – that is, those without a large domestic market for their products – are the most vulnerable.

The current trend of using financial market criteria as a means of judging a country's economic health also leads to narrowly focused and short-term thinking and planning. It ignores the long-term problems in a country and the social and environmental problems that may undermine an entire society. For the financial speculator, however, a country in trouble is just another market to be wary about, and at the same time, a potential source of fast and easy profits.

The future: will it be a repeat of the recent past?

While current patterns of globalization seem unlikely to change dramatically in the next few years or even decades, there were initial signs that, especially in the light of the crisis in East Asia, some attempts to regulate the global system were likely. There is now, at least at a rhetorical level, a broad consensus on three issues: that general worldwide standards of living must be improved; that globalization must be transformed from a process of exclusion to one of inclusion; and that new international norms and multilateral institutions need to be developed to enable global and democratic governance.

Such proposals as have been made draw partly on America's New Deal experience after the Great Depression of 1929, arguing that global capitalism can be humanized and harnessed for the good of humanity. Since it is unlikely that a New Deal of the 1930s variety will be adequate in the current global context, like-minded civil society groups in all countries must concentrate on alliance-building to develop an agenda that is a genuine alternative to current patterns and processes of global capitalism, not merely a 21st-century version of the New Deal.

The problem and its history

The boom-and-bust cycle is not a malfunction of an otherwise perfect system – it is intrinsic to capitalism. A healthy economy attracts investors; profitable returns attract riskier speculation; eventually the economy cannot sustain this pattern and decline quickly follows. The appearance of speculative mania before the onset of a crisis is a common factor in all crises.

In comparing the Mexican crisis with the East Asian one, analysts often like to emphasize that the Asian crisis was essentially related to private debts while the Mexican one was a public debt crisis. However, in our view this is merely a difference of presentation. The Mexican crisis was caused by speculation following the government's raising of interest rates to attract foreign investment. The consequent inflation combined with other factors to produce instability and market panic.

The Southeast Asian crisis

In the mid-1980s, Japanese companies began to invest heavily in Southeast Asian countries. When the Japanese economy began to decline in the early 1990s, those countries sought other investors to enable their investment-led growth to continue. To attract investment, they liberalized their capital accounts and raised interest rates, encouraged all along by international approval. At the height of the boom in 1997, just before the bust, the World

Bank commented approvingly that 'the surge in flows reflected these countries' strong economic performance, including rapid growth, sustained improvements in macroeconomic balances, and structural changes that have fostered a market-led, outward orientation since the late 1980s'. In the troubled days of 1998 the Bank's tone changed, and it noted that the region suffered from 'large current account deficits and misallocated investment, bad loans and currency and maturity mismatches, and misaligned real exchange rates and lost competitiveness' – as if these problems had not been present before.

The investment had mostly been channelled into the short-term, high-yield areas of stock markets, consumer credit and real estate. Investment in the production of goods and services, which is always a more long-term project and involves commitment in a particular place, was less attractive because of the cumulative impact of a supply-side economy that had resulted in oversupply and corresponding low profitability margins in the real economy.

Between July 1997 and January 1998, the region's currencies fell in value by an average of about 40 per cent. The worst-affected countries, Indonesia and Thailand, were those that did not have advanced, stable economies, but were in transition from agricultural to more industrialized economies, resulting in a situation wherein the sudden reversal of fortunes hit the poorer sections of the population hardest. Unemployment rose sharply, and rural areas in Thailand, for example, could not cope with the reverse migration and lack of remittances of people returning from the cities. Crime rates rose, and children who would have been in school were forced to look for work at whatever wages they could get.

When the governments took the internationally prescribed steps to deal with their economic problems, they exacerbated the plight of the worst-off by cutting back public expenditures and increasing indirect taxes. Not only were these measures endorsed by the international financial community, but in fact the IMF had stipulated such actions as conditions for its assistance.

Many TNCs also suffered, but many gained, taking advantage of distress sales of assets that others had to sell at bargain-basement prices. They were also able to employ labour at lower wages than before. Others cut their losses and moved abroad to wherever conditions were more amenable. In general the situation in Southeast Asia for TNCs became even better than it had been before the crisis. As Robert Hormat of Goldman Sachs dared to say, 'thanks in part to the Asian crisis, we are in the midst of the most competitive environment in world history.' The use of the term 'competitive' in this context was a euphemistic reference to the bargain-basement prices that companies such as Goldman Sachs got away with paying for their new acquisitions in the crisis countries.

The right remedies?

The IMF's rescue programmes, with their conditions of further market liberalization, found ready takers in Thailand. In Southeast Asia, Indonesia and especially Malaysia were less keen to embrace the IMF's conditions. Malaysia, in fact, refused to allow such external interference in its economic policies. President Suharto of Indonesia also initially defied the IMF and announced increased subsidies for petrol and staples, and a big increase in government spending. The IMF's relentless pressure, tied to its bail-out resources, however, forced him to relent and introduce economic stringencies that provoked riots and unrest throughout Indonesia, eventually leading to his resignation.

The stabilization programmes led by the IMF came under criticism for a number of reasons. The most important of these included:

- The prescribed public-sector medicine was inappropriate for the private-debt crisis in Asia. Austerity in the public sector actually exacerbated economic problems, allowing no relief to those people who were most negatively affected by the crisis.

- The IMF unjustly and inappropriately interfered with the domestic economic policies of sovereign countries. One effect of the exposure of these countries' economies to the IMF 'rescue' packages has been to further lessen their control over their domestic affairs.

- The IMF often ignored, and hence exacerbated, particular local problems. It also ignored the fact that developing countries, by definition, are not at a stage of development appropriate for the type of economic and financial liberalization policies undertaken by industrialized Western countries.

- Ironically, the IMF's programmes had the effect of benefiting TNCs at the expense of the host countries, although it was largely the activities of TNCs that had caused the crisis in the first place.

- The crisis demonstrated the inability of the IMF to foresee problems or solve them after they occur. Although the IMF insists on transparency within governments, its own procedures and decision-making processes remain secretive.

- In the eyes of the affected countries, the IMF often appears to act at the behest of the West and particularly the United States and its Treasury. This has exacerbated tensions between East and West.

Pros and cons of unregulated capital flows

Despite the Asian-led global crisis, capital account liberalization remains one of the fundamental aims of the IMF, even if it has for political reasons been temporarily relegated to the backburner. Nevertheless, until the collapse of the Bretton Woods system in the early 1970s, exchange and capital controls were considered a normal and necessary part of each country's economic policy armoury. Especially for smaller countries, controls ensured stability, and allowed governments to pursue policies in the national interest – such as full employment or protection of key industries. Above all, they reflected the principle that each country was responsible for the management of its national economy. Financial systems were thus made consistent with national objectives and, in the economic sphere at least, individual freedom was not promoted at the expense of social needs.

In the 1970s, economic thinking around the world began to change. It was argued that economic interventions by the state distorted the general equilibrium and the workings of the market and were economically inefficient and ineffective in maximizing general welfare. They were believed to benefit special interest groups at the expense of the general population and, in some instances, to lead to wholesale corruption. Countries around the world, attracted by neo-liberal economic theory, which appeared to promise both greater prosperity and greater freedom, loosened economic regulation and control. They gave far too little weight to the need for sound fiscal and monetary policy and proper regulatory oversight of the financial system *before* the introduction of economic liberalization.

In the light of the crises in Mexico and Southeast Asia in the 1990s, some of the advocates of liberalization have begun to recognize the speculative and destabilizing tendencies of the prevailing model. They have noted that free movement of capital could lead to herding behaviour by investors and the consequent inflow and outflow of capital in quantities that adversely affect national and local economies. No matter how well-managed such economies are, they cannot cope with the magnitude and the quick pace of such outflows.

One other disturbing phenomenon is worth highlighting. We have seen in recent years a proliferation of policies and legal measures designed to reinforce the rights and political representation of investors, and in so doing to strengthen the global power of capital. This is what Stephen Gill has called the 'new constitutionalism'.

Many commentators argue that offshore financial centres and tax havens are one striking manifestation of this trend. Jurisdictions have emerged from new and evasive practices that are not subject to the reach of the state. Others see such 'offshores' as 'a radical redrawing of state sovereignty' not its erosion. For example, it is only a state that, through legislative acts, can create offshore financial centres.

While this may be true in a technical sense, there can be no denying that such arrogation of control by corporations, banks and other financial enterprises provides them with new opportunities to manage capital flows in ways which may be both inequitable and unaccountable. States – and nations – are as a result losing the capacity to oversee transactions, acquire revenue and manage institutions in ways that are contrary to any notion of democratic governance. At some point, these offshore spaces and their related global markets, though initially created by the state, come to exercise rights of movement and decision-making which escape the control of states, especially in developing countries but even in middle-sized industrialized countries.

Challenging mainstream views

The basic assumptions behind the financial and economic liberalization model remain largely unquestioned despite the recent crises. Speculative behaviour is the main destabilizing factor, and it can be considered intrinsic to the system because investors regard such behaviour as rational. Performing risky and speculative transactions, for example, has its rationale in the prospect of high returns.

For Keynesian analysts, global integration of markets should proceed, but only in conjunction with adequate checks and balances. Under Keynesian prescriptions, each country needs to get its economic fundamentals right and ensure a sustainable domestic economy and a system of supervision of the activities of financial institutions. The state should regain control of capital flows in order to ensure both national economic sovereignty and the ability to pursue economic policies in the national interest. The citizens of a country, rather than international or even local, financial interests, should control the nation's economy.

The objection that re-regulation would restrict the ability of developing countries to attract the capital they need to finance their development can be dismissed on two counts. First, it is questionable whether the gains from capital inflows into developing countries have been sustainable and outweighed the drawbacks, which include their tendency to destabilize countries. Second, capital flows operate both ways, and the net transfers of capital to developing countries have often been insignificant.

Structural-Marxist analysts, on the other hand, repudiate the attempt to attain global market integration as an end in itself. For such analysts, this is merely a continuation of the capitalist model that delayed sound development in all countries for centuries. Many of them believe that countries need to de-link themselves from international markets and pursue profound nationally-oriented restructuring of their economies.

Proposed and existing mechanisms for regulation

In the wake of the Asian crisis, the international financial community has come up with several proposals for reforming the global economic system. Few have involved substantial structural reform.

The most influential position is that of the US government. Early on in the crisis, it identified the main problems as the related ones of lack of transparency and the dominance of crony capitalism at the national level. This analysis was compatible with the IMF's analysis and the basis of its rescue programmes, which emphasized transparency along with continued liberalization as the solution to the crisis, together with fiscal austerity and monetary conservatism.

The US administration has since advocated four basic ideas for reform of the international financial system: increased openness; strengthened national financial systems; more soundly-based capital flows in industrial nations; and new ways to respond to crises, with a greater role for the private sector in creating rescue packages. These general ideas have not been matched by specific proposals. No action is envisaged to control hedge funds, or to increase national regulation over capital flows. The US position in fact goes further than mere compatibility with IMF policy since many believed that it was the US Treasury that significantly influenced the IMF response to the crisis.

The Group of Seven (G7) proposals, despite initial differences between the positions of the United States, Germany and France, were in the end predominantly influenced by the United States. One proposal was for a strengthened role for the IMF as a lender of last resort. A US$90 billion fund, under the direction of the IMF, was proposed, to avoid the recurrence of crises like the Asian one of the late 1990s. The IMF would be expected to use the fund as lender of last resort to pre-empt or forestall the desta-bilizing conditions that lead to crises. Critics have pointed out that this fund, as proposed, presents a moral hazard since it resembles a safety net for speculators, and is therefore unlikely to deter the riskier forms of profit-seeking that lead to crises in the first place.

Again like the United States, the G7 continues to argue for greater transparency. While it called for an examination of the operations of hedge funds with a view to getting them to 'comply with internationally agreed standards', it was short of specific suggestions beyond recommending that the IMF should do more and oversee everything.

One new institutional mechanism that emerged from G7 discussions was the creation, in 1999, of the Financial Stability Forum which is based in the Bank of International Settlements in Basle, Switzerland. The Forum consists of G7 finance ministry officials and central bankers, representatives of the IMF, the World Bank, and other international bodies. It does not include representatives from developing countries – the countries most vulnerable to the sorts of crises the Forum is supposedly set up to prevent. Its basic objectives are threefold: to assess vulnerabilities in the international financial system; to identify and oversee action to deal with those vulnerabilities; and to improve co-ordination and communication among the various authorities responsible for financial stability.

Another proposal which has yet to be acted upon but which deserves particular attention is the one presented by the Chancellor of the Exchequer, Gordon Brown, for 'a new IMF surveillance unit'. This recommendation for an enhanced surveillance role for the IMF could indeed be useful if such surveillance was seriously directed at the industrialized countries from which the vast majority of capital flows emanate.

Issues in control and regulation

Banking regulation and prudential norms. Existing standards for banking activity were designed for banks in the advanced economies. They have proven to be less than adequate for some of the transactions within the global banking system, especially for those involving developing economies. They are also unsuitable for adequately dealing with recent developments such as derivatives.

Regulating hedge funds and other highly-leveraged institutions. The recent rise of powerful, highly-leveraged but largely unregulated global investment funds has led to the need to find some way of fitting them into a more sound world financial system. Transparency is one key proposal; others have yet to be determined as the world financial community tries to come to terms with this development.

Regulating capital flows. Perhaps the main danger posed by large capital inflows is that a resulting appreciation of the exchange rate can destabilize a local economy, and attempts to alleviate the situation can prove counter-productive. Chile has tried to deal with this problem while allowing foreign direct investment to continue. The principal components of the Chilean system are:

- sterilized intervention to prevent excessive appreciation of the exchange rate;
- investment regulations specifying a minimum period during which capital cannot be repatriated;

- a reserve requirement of 30 per cent on short-term investments to discourage speculative inflows.

This model has received considerable attention. Its main drawback may be that it depends on a range of economic and institutional factors which may not exist in every country, and it therefore needs to be adapted to local circumstances, if it can be adapted at all.

In Malaysia, in response to the 1998 crisis, the government ignored the standard IMF prescription of raising interest rates and introducing austerity measures, and instead attempted to pump-prime the economy back to life, control capital outflows and peg the ringgit's exchange value to the US dollar. Despite predictions of disaster, the measures appear to have worked, and when restrictions on outflows were lifted a year later, little money had actually left Malaysia.

Once again, the success of this strategy has drawn considerable international attention. However, it should be noted that the other affected countries in Southeast Asia have also begun to recover, admittedly to varying degrees, even though they followed IMF prescriptions.

Transparency and accountability. There is no doubt that the lack of transparency and accountability in financial dealings has played a big part in recent episodes of economic instability. A report from the Group of 22 (G22) defines transparency as 'a process by which information about existing conditions, decisions and actions is made accessible, visible and understandable', and accountability as recognition of 'the need to justify and accept responsibility for decisions taken'. The report notes that all three major players must practise these virtues: the private sector, national authorities and international financial institutions (IFIs).

International standards. The IMF has taken steps to promote and implement internationally accepted codes and standards, with the aim of producing a more open and efficient international financial system. Transparency is the central theme of these proposals, and the IMF has prepared experimental case studies which examine transparency practices. Other international bodies are also working on standards, including the areas of accounting and auditing, corporate governance and regulation of securities markets.

Taxes on foreign exchange transactions

The Tobin Tax. A tax on international currency transactions, proposed by James Tobin in 1978, has gained in attraction in the intervening years, as international currency flows have grown exponentially and international bodies have looked for new sources of income to meet the increased demand for various forms of international activity. The probable tax would be between 0.1 and 0.25 per cent, applied to all foreign-exchange transactions, although a much higher rate of 1 per cent has been proposed if the tax is to have a real impact on short-term speculative activity. The effect on long-term investment of such a higher taxation rate would be minimal on long-term foreign direct investment while its enormous cumulative effect on profit would act as a restraint on short-term flows while simultaneously yielding considerable revenues for the recipients of the tax.

Among the likely advantages of the Tobin Tax or modified currency transactions tax are the following:

- it would effectively discourage short-term speculative flows;
- it has great potential for revenue creation, especially for use in international financial distress;
- it would contribute to the generation of foreign exchange reserves;
- it could help stabilize international currency flows;
- it alters incentives, rather than relying on command and control mechanisms.

Its critics, however, cite the following reasons against such a tax:

- its technical feasibility is questionable;
- it will be evaded;
- it may provoke the creation of new instruments of avoidance;
- it may distort market behaviour;
- it would require the creation of a new supranational authority that national authorities might not accept.

In answer to these criticisms, the tax's proponents have argued that the tax would be feasible if applied at the national level, at the intermediate, netting stage of foreign exchange transactions, and it could even be imposed unilaterally by any country on all transactions involving its currency. The question of evasion has not yet been dealt with; 80 per cent of transactions, however, currently involve major countries, which could easily agree on implementation.

While cost may be a deterrent to the establishment of new instruments, any distortion of market behaviour would only be in the direction of deterring undesirable activity. Existing authorities could oversee the tax; national bodies, weighing the overall costs of the tax against the costs of continuing without it, would be likely to decide in favour, especially if they can keep some of the revenues generated for their own national-level activities.

A cross-border payments tax. A cross-border payments tax would fall within the jurisdiction of the country levying it and not depend on any global agreement. However, it would mostly deal with current account rather than capital account transactions, which would limit its effectiveness in handling capital flows.

Taxes on short-term profits. A levy has been proposed on profits from investments held for less than a year, and an end to tax deductions on short-term losses.

Domestic financial transaction tax. A tax on all financial transactions was first proposed by Keynes, and has been further elaborated by Tobin. It would apply only to domestic transactions and the scope of its coverage would be up to each country. Many countries already levy a similar tax, especially on share transactions.

Renewing the governance of the global economy

The Asian crisis has provided an important opportunity for the world community to look at the developments and shortcomings of the present global economic system, including its broader political and social impact, efficiency and integrity. Few analysts have expressed continued faith in the system as it stands.

GENERAL PRINCIPLES

Sustainable Human and Social Development. The pursuit of economic growth as a primary aim, or even of economic growth with equity, is not enough. Sustainable human and social development should *include* economic growth, but that growth should come about *through* equity.

The dominant view focuses on shortages of income as the main indicator of poverty, but a comprehensive notion of poverty encompasses much more. For example, the UNDP's 1997 *Human Development Report* focused on 'the denial of opportunities and choices most basic to human development – to lead a long, healthy, creative life and to enjoy a decent standard of living, freedom, self-esteem and the respect of others'. The human-development understanding of poverty sees it 'not as a condition but as a process'.

When we speak of growth we need to ask: Growth of what and for what? All sorts of socially damaging activities can contribute to economic growth as it is usually measured – consumer luxuries, prostitution, drug-trafficking – whereas socially valuable activities, such as education, environmental regeneration, justice and democratic participation, may not contribute at all to such 'growth'. Questions about quality are asked less often than questions about quantity.

The primary challenge of sustainable development is to make economic policy-making accountable to human development and social-policy goals.

Accountability. Since the collapse of the Bretton Woods system in the early 1970s, two trends have developed in parallel: slower growth rates among the richer nations, and an exponential growth of the financial sector. Along with the growth of international finance has come far greater volatility in the world economic system. These trends suggest that two other crucial forms of accountability are also needed to enable a fundamental renewal of governance of the global economy: first, global mechanisms must be made accountable to those at local, national and regional level, following the principle of subsidiarity; second, the financial 'bubble' economy must exist to serve the real, productive economy at all four levels.

In line with the principle of subsidiarity what can be achieved or decided at the local level should not be done at the national level; what should be decided at the national level should not be imposed from the regional level; and what can be done at the regional level should not be done at the global level. Furthermore, national and regional arrangements should be the foundation and building blocks for global institutions and arrangements rather than the other way around.

Such genuine accountability will imply a very different form of economic and political governance from the prevailing neo-liberal one. A fundamental tenet of the economy should be that the financial system, and economic and financial policies more generally, are means to sustainable human development and not an end in themselves. Several principles follow from this one:

- There should be recognition of the indivisibility of economic, social and political rights, policies and governance issues and no artificial separation or compartmentalization of these.

- Making national, regional and global governance mechanisms more participatory and accountable to citizens is both desirable and necessary for the achievement of sustainable human development.

- A greater role in economic and social policy issues needs to be played by the United Nations (as a relatively more democratic and representative body) than is played by the Bretton Woods institutions and the WTO.

While all four levels of governance – local, national, regional and global – are necessary, and the importance of governance at sub-national levels should not be underestimated, this section gives pre-eminence to issues at the national, regional and global levels, which hold the greatest potential to counteract global forces in favour of the common good.

The national level

Economic governance implications. At a national level, a key requirement of the renewal of economic governance will be an increase in national autonomy in policy choice by states and their governments. Equally important is the need to increase the efficiency of markets to promote greater national macroeconomic policy autonomy and financial stability. Such an approach will necessitate the following:

- a monetary policy that responds primarily to the needs of households and small-to-medium-scale enterprises, rather than to players in the global economy;
- a fiscal policy framework based on a progressive direct taxation system instead of the minimalist and regressive tax regimes that currently prevail. Only such a framework can provide the resources for sustaining comprehensive social policy and human development projects;
- an economic policy rooted in domestic savings and the domestic market, rather than one relying on foreign capital;
- a discriminating approach to foreign financial flows, concentrating on those that promise to contribute to the production of useful goods and services and the creation of employment;
- the use of national-level capital controls, selectively applied, as an essential element of economic governance. Such controls can ensure that a country's foreign exchange inflows and outflows are neither mismatched nor excessive.

Political governance implications. The current global crisis has reinforced the idea that economic and political governance are inseparable, and that good economic governance depends as much, or more, on good political governance at all levels as on sound economic fundamentals.

The demands of better and more sustainable political governance pose at least two related challenges: first, the need to move beyond electoral democracy to more popular forms of transparent and accountable democracy; and second, the need to consider issues of process and participation much more seriously than in the past. Civil society will need to be strengthened and institutionalized at all levels of political activity.

Roles of the state and civil society. In recent years governments have transferred some of their activities to CSOs, or have cut back their activities and left a gap that CSOs have been obliged to try to fill, even though this has not always been appropriate. The strengths of CSOs do not lie in the sorts of large-scale service delivery required in areas such as health, education, power and water. Only governments can operate on the scale necessary for such service provision if a serious dent in poverty reduction is to be made. CSOs must play an important role, but their main value lies in the important societal watchdog function that the best of them play so well. Some of them are also an excellent source of innovative ideas on substantive areas of work, ranging from globalization, and trade and debt reduction to conflict transformation, peacebuilding, human rights protection, and enhancement of vulnerable population groups. The *raison d'être* of CSOs committed to democratization and development initiatives will, however, lie in their monitoring, criticizing and public-policy-influencing roles. Where appropriate, they should also support strengthening the role of the state (such as in the provision of core public goods) and particular governments.

The state and civil society may be considered as two sides of the coin of balanced governance. Each has its indispensable role on which the other should not encroach, but each needs both the support and the criticism of the other. Each is a fundamental part of democracy. Without a strong civil society, the state becomes unaccountable; without a strong state, civil society has no firm basis for its operation, and sustained and significant poverty eradication will be an unattainable goal.

It is an essential part of the role of CSOs that they represent the interests of the poor and vulnerable population groups, particularly in a climate such as the present one where governments have abdicated some of their social responsibilities. While this may involve direct action, it must not be as a long-term substitute for the proper role of the state, and CSOs must make this clear to governments. Rather, CSOs should see part of their role as building awareness within society of the need for the state to accept its responsibilities, and organize citizens in order to bring this about.

As to the state, in an era of globalization it is of the utmost importance for it to develop its capacity to regulate and constrain the power and reach of IFIs and TNCs in order to maintain local and national autonomy. Numerous recent examples have shown that a move towards the market is not necessarily a move towards freedom and prosperity. Without a strong state, market liberalization can be the road to ruin.

The state has the responsibility to build and maintain a social security system that provides genuine security for its citizens. Equally, only the state can ensure that a country's education system meets the needs of the people in both the short and long terms. The state also has a central role in both designing crisis-response programmes and in forestalling future crises. Building sustained local institutional capacity in financial, economic, political and social governance areas is also likely to be an unavoidable objective if a country is to make strides towards achieving sustainable human development. Only when such an institutional framework is strong and working well should further economic and financial liberalization be considered.

Above all, it must be recognized that regulation, however effective and comprehensive, is not a substitute for the performance of all these important roles of government. In the current globalizing economy much more than regulation, however effective, will be needed.

The regional level

The importance of existing and new regional and sub-regional governance and consultation mechanisms and organizations will be crucial in the context of accelerating globalization and the increasing number of issues that can no longer be dealt with at the national level. The global and regional context is of crucial and increasing importance in terms of defining the space that is available for action at the national level. This is because it has become difficult, if not impossible, to manage national economies without paying attention to larger regional and global economic forces, policies, laws and agreements.

Despite this, at the moment, the regional level of governance is the weakest. It is thus a matter of great urgency that this change in a manner which will allow developing countries and CSOs to exert a greater influence from the regional to the global level rather than the other way around, which is too often the case at present.

Inter-governmental regional groupings and mechanisms. While groupings such as the Association of Southeast Asian Nations (ASEAN), the European Union (EU) and the Southern Common Market (MERCOSUR) have achieved some successes in this regard, the record of inter-governmental regional bodies as intermediary, mediating or countervailing layers of governance, which are supportive of the national or local levels against the global, is far from satisfactory. Sometimes, as with the North American Free Trade Association (NAFTA) and the Asia Pacific Economic Co-operation group (APEC), they have appeared to be little more than handmaidens of global institutions. However, there are signs that both the EU (with the creation of the Euro) and ASEAN or a larger East Asian grouping (in the wake of the Asian crisis) may exert more independence for the common regional good.

Regional civil society initiatives. As with governments, civil society groupings are weakest at the regional level. While regional initiatives such as Common Frontiers as a response to NAFTA in North America are important examples of crucial civil society initiatives on economic governance issues, there is a need to strengthen and multiply regional and sub-regional civil society groupings on these issues and move further from critiques to the articulation of alternatives to the current structures of global and political governance. A dual strategy of critique and articulation of alternatives will be crucial for sustaining a strong, coherent and influential civil society voice on the key emerging issues of global economic governance.

The global level

No matter what action is taken at national or regional levels, local and national economies will still be vulnerable to the global economy unless action is taken at a global level as well. The principle that should underlie the creation of mechanisms and institutions of global governance is that they should be enabling and supportive of national and regional efforts rather than attempting to dominate them. Equally important is the principle that reform at the global level should involve the full participation of civil society.

Accountability of the Bretton Woods institutions to a reformed UN system. The Bretton Woods institutions were originally intended to serve as arms of the United Nations, yet they have had their own, much less democratic governance mechanisms and largely followed their own agendas. If the governance of the global economy is to be renewed, as it must, then the centre of gravity has to move away from these narrowly-focused financial and economic institutions, to the more human development-centred institutions of the non-Bretton Woods UN system. Despite the shortcomings of the UN system as it stands, it is still in the best position to deal with the current dysfunctional and unbalanced system of global governance. If it undergoes the reforms outlined in this report, either beforehand or simultaneously, it would be even better placed to make the IFIs more accountable and more sensitive to the needs and expectations of civil society.

Civil society action at the global level. Civil society campaigns and proposals for global governance are much more plentiful than at the national level, covering issues such as reform or abolition of the World Bank, IMF and WTO, defeat of the OECD's Multilateral Agreement on Investment (MAI) and the abolition of landmines. In addition to keeping up the pressure of critique, CSOs will need to ensure that they prioritize the formulation of a cohesive and comprehensive articulation of alternatives for global economic and political governance. Equally, they will need to take full advantage of the new institutional opportunities as these are progressively realized over the coming years.

In concluding this outline of principles, it cannot be overemphasized that sustainable human development will remain a distant dream unless we can collectively gather the political will to make the necessary bold and radical changes to the existing system and institutions of global economic governance. The way to start is by ensuring the three forms of accountability outlined earlier by re-subordinating the financial system to the real economy, subordinating macro and other economic policy to social and human development objectives, and subordinating the global level of governance to the local, regional, and especially the national levels.

INITIATIVES

The national level

- National implementation of a Currency Transactions Tax on international foreign exchange transactions within the framework of an international co-operation agreement. This tax will need to be at a level sufficient to serve as a disincentive for speculators and should be focused on short-term capital flows. An incentive system whereby revenues generated from such a tax can be used partially at the national level, partially at the regional level and partially at the global level, will need to underpin the tax.

  Such a tax, which would be levied at the national level but would apply to currency transactions of non-residents of countries participating in the international taxation agreement at a higher rate than residents of participating countries, does not need universal adoption or even the initial participation of all the major global financial centres to work. It could start in a first phase (short to medium term) with countries such as Canada (whose parliament has voted for such a tax) and others on a voluntary basis who would establish, initially, an open but non-binding international co-operation agreement – that is, any state can join at any time but no one will be forced to join. This would be the short-term objective.

- A new supranational body, an *International Taxation Organization* (ITO), should take responsibility for the collection and allocation of revenues. Its governing council should be made up only of representatives of tax-imposing governments who would be responsible for deciding the allocation and use of the tax revenues generated. It is recommended that allocations be split three ways, with approximately one-third going to the national, regional and global levels, but that criteria for the use of tax revenue (to be approved by the governing council) should be designed to facilitate the achievement of the 2015 international goals and targets of poverty eradication.

The one-third allocation for the national level should provide a strong incentive for governments to participate. Allocations at the global level should give priority to the UN, and at the regional level to organizations that encompass and seek the mutual advancement of all countries within a given region. Such a distribution of revenues should make it possible for the UN, for example, to establish much greater independence than it currently has from some of its most powerful and richest members.

In its formative stage, the ITO should maintain its full independence from existing global governance mechanisms including the UN, both because of its non-universal character and because such independence will help it achieve its tasks in its formative years. In the medium to long term, especially as its membership becomes more universal, it should be accountable to the proposed Economic and Social Security Council (see below).

It is hoped that the ITO will create the political pressure for most UN member states to join it once it establishes itself. This is for a number of reasons including the fact that, if states do not join, their residents, as non-residents of tax-imposing states, will continue to pay higher taxes than residents of tax-imposing states for currency transactions in those states and their governments will be excluded from decision-making about tax allocations at both the regional and global levels.

- The proposed currency transactions tax and the International Taxation Organization would have the added advantage of beginning to apply a brake on the major problem of unregulated offshore financial centres. An important first step in the internationally co-ordinated state action envisaged here is the proposed phasing, with a voluntary first phase in which financial transactions in non-participating states are taxed at a higher rate than those in participating states.

- Other attempts to enhance the effectiveness of national economic management would include:
  o regulations to increase the reporting requirements of investors, especially hedge funds, which are currently exempt from these. This recommendation should not require detailed elaboration;
  o regulations to increase the surveillance of capital flows, especially from industrialized countries. In the short term, this task may need

to be performed by the IMF whose Charter mandate requires it to do this. In the longer term, however, this task should become the responsibility of the WFA (see below);

o capital controls at the national level, especially on inflows. These should be phased out in a gradual manner if and when the institutional framework to effectively manage such a phasing-out is in place at national, regional and global levels as part of a coherent and comprehensive world financial framework.

The regional level

- Creation of regional, or where appropriate, sub-regional institutions or arrangements (e.g. *East Asian Monetary Fund*). These would not just be new 'funds' in existing institutions but new institutions at a regional or sub-regional level, as appropriate. The objective would be both to have institutions that are more responsive to regional and country-specific realities and differences, and to encourage greater competition and pluralism in monetary and fiscal policy choice in times of crisis.

Such institutions should be tripartite in their composition and membership, which should be limited to countries in that sub-region or region as far as possible. They should have governmental, CSO and private-sector participation although only governments should have voting powers, based on democratic principles and no exercise of a veto.

The long-term objective would be to have such regional or sub-regional institutions in all continents. However, in the short to medium term, regions with a large number of 'emerging market' countries, such as East Asia and certain sub-regions of Latin America, should be prioritized. This is both because of the urgent need and realistic possibility of establishing such institutions in these regions.

For example, such an arrangement is realistically possible in East Asia in three to five years' time because both the resources to underwrite such a sub-regional or even regional Fund through accumulated foreign exchange reserves and the institutional capacity to create it exist in the sub-region itself. This may be less true for other developing-country regions, but the establishment of such an institution is feasible in both South Asia and parts of Latin America in the medium term, while it may take longer to achieve in sub-Saharan Africa. A two- to five-year timetable is definitely possible for East Asia while five to ten years should be the target for both South Asia and Latin America.

The global level

• Establishment of a coherent, consistent and comprehensive world financial framework in the short to medium term, and as a first step towards the realization of global coordination of financial mechanisms and institutions. Such a framework should encompass institutions and arrangements at the national, regional and global levels. The guiding principle of such a framework should be that of subsidiarity, and its processes should be guided by national and regional processes and institutions. Unlike in the case of previous proposals, no additional institutions or new legal entity (other than the proposed ITO) are being suggested at the global level, at least in the short term.

The process of establishing such a coherent and consistent framework should be facilitated by a series of meetings at the regional and global levels. Given the experience, processes and power realities of the recently-created WTO, this world financial framework should not be formalized as a global institution in the short to medium term. National, sub-regional and regional processes should be the priority to establish and strengthen in the next two- to ten-year period. This should lead to both trust and the possibility of building a World Financial Authority from the 'bottom up' over the long term.

• The formalization of a world financial framework should in the longer term take shape through the creation of a *World Financial Authority* (WFA) under the auspices of the UN, but only if the experience of the short to medium term has been positive. This will imply the need for monitoring and evaluation of the world financial framework over the short to medium term.

In the long term, the WFA should make the existence of international financial institutions such as the IMF and the Bank for International Settlements (BIS) redundant. Once regional monetary funds (e.g. East Asian Monetary Fund) and financial mechanisms are functioning effectively, the remaining limited functions still fulfilled by these IFIs could in fact be absorbed by the WFA, under much greater democratic accountability than currently exists or is ever likely in the case of either the IMF or BIS. The IMF and BIS should be closed down if the WFA has taken over their functions. If not, they should be accountable to the WFA. The aim must be to place the workings of the international financial system under full public scrutiny, and to give all of the world's governments and the diverse voices that comprise the emerging global civil society the opportunity to shape future directions and priorities.

The WFA, when created, will have to act as the overall regulator of global finance at the global level and would have executive powers and the authority to impose mandatory sanctions. It would also have to be established in a democratically accountable manner with a mandate from the General Assembly and accountable to a revitalized and reformed Economic and Social Council (ECOSOC) or its successor institution.

The WFA should exercise regulatory oversight and other governance functions over the global financial system and its institutions. Such a body is urgently required both to prevent and deal with the sorts of economic crises that have been a feature of recent years. Its fundamental brief would be to ensure world economic conditions that enable growth, redistribution, employment and stability. It must establish regulatory mechanisms that are international and enforceable. It would need to minimize systemic risk arising from the operations of financial markets and develop policies to manage such risk.

In order for the Authority to work it would need the co-operation and support of national monetary and financial authorities. There has already been a great deal of fruitful international co-operation in the area of money laundering, and there would appear to be no reason why this cannot be extended to other areas of antisocial international financial activity. Both the technical and international co-operation requirements of dealing with money-laundering and capital flight are broadly similar; the current difference lies largely in the first being regarded as an undesirable activity while flows of the latter kind are indiscriminately regarded as desirable.

National governments, in consultation with the Authority, would be able to impose restrictions on external capital movements, and the Authority would be empowered to ensure that the controls of one country are not subverted by others. To achieve these aims, the WFA would need executive authority with surveillance and enforcement capabilities. The fact that the WTO has been created with such powers shows what can be achieved in this area if the political will exists to exercise them in a desirable direction.

- IMF reform involves three priority recommendations in the short to medium term:
  - limiting IMF operations to their original narrow mandate of surveillance and stabilization should be a short- to medium-term priority (two to five years). This will imply a phasing out, for example, of the Enhanced Structural Adjustment Facility (ESAF – recently renamed the Poverty Reduction and Growth Facility: PRGF);

     ○ ensuring that there is no change to its Charter mandate on capital account convertibility; establishing instead that it strictly enforces the current Charter article relating to controls on the capital account;

     ○ universal implementation of its surveillance role, with particular emphasis on the implementation of this role *vis-à-vis* industrialized countries, which are the origin of the vast majority of global capital flows. The IMF should be tasked with surveillance of both the volume of capital flows and their specific composition and destination in the short to medium term (until the WFA takes over this function in the long term).

- An *International Independent Debt Arbitration Mechanism* should be created under the broad auspices of the United Nations. Such a mechanism should address the invidious current situation where creditors are also the arbiters and unilateral judges of debt. Such a Mechanism should also be tasked with identifying different categories of debt (e.g. odious, illegitimate, honorific) and ruling on those categories that should be cancelled as well as those that need to be repaid. It should also identify the conditions, priority and timeframe for such repayments.

- Serious consideration should be given to the creation of an *International Bankruptcy Court*, constituted along the lines of Chapter XI of US bankruptcy law.

- Most important is the creation of a new, broadly based *Economic and Social Security Council* as a principal entity of the United Nations (comparable in status to the Security Council), accountable to the General Assembly. While in the short to medium term this should build on ECOSOC, in the longer term it should supersede this body. The proposed People's Assembly and Consultative Assembly should also be represented in the Economic and Social Security Council in the long term, although voting power should lie only with state members.

In the short term and as an intermediate step, the existing ECOSOC should be upgraded. Some steps that would assist this could include holding more frequent and more focused meetings. It should, for example, meet to discuss specific economic and social issues such as a financial crisis or a significant globalization trend that warrants attention. This could result in a meeting for a day every couple of months.

Another short-term reform should be a strengthening of the role of the Bureau (the executive). The Bureau should meet whenever the Chair judged this to be necessary to discuss both substantive and procedural issues, as do the Bureaux of other bodies such as the

ECOSOC commissions – the Commissions on Social Development and Sustainable Development. If these meetings were sufficiently frequent and substantive, they would change both the nature of ECOSOC deliberations and country representation for the better.

Such modest changes in the short term could be achieved by ambitious use of the powers already available, if these are exercised on the basis of a decision by the existing bodies and initial moves through the leadership of the Chair. They would be significant changes in their own right and would lay the groundwork for the more ambitious changes recommended in the medium to long term.

In the longer term, the powers and mandate of ECOSOC need to be enlarged, and its name should be changed to Economic and Social Security Council.

The powers of this Council should be expanded to include a summoning power to ensure a certain degree of accountability of all the key actors, monitoring, research and analysis, advocacy and a regular rapporteur responsibility. Its mandate should be expanded to include all the economic, financial and social systemic issues (e.g. debt, trade, finance, private capital flows, ODA) likely to be included in the agenda of the proposed high-level inter-governmental ministerial gathering currently under consideration for 2001 and with a focus on the financing of development.

The specialized agencies of the UN, the Bretton Woods institutions and the WTO would all have to respond to any summons served on them by Council members, as would non-state actors such as TNCs and CSOs. This would not imply any power to direct the policy of these bodies, but as in the case of the US Congress, Standing Committees of the Council could be created for a number of broad policy areas (e.g. finance, trade).

In addition, *ad hoc* subcommittees could be formed to examine specific issues arising out of particular developments (e.g. a specific financial crisis).

Standing and *ad hoc* committees of the Council would have the power not only to summon officials and experts, but to issue periodic reports outlining the testimony, providing research and analysis by committee staff and making non-binding policy recommendations to the UN General Assembly, IMF, World Bank, WTO and other relevant organizations which would be expected to act on the recommendations made.

While the Council, at least in the medium term, may not have any enforcement or sanction capability over the institutions to which it makes recommendations for action, it will be able to use its power of summons to call on these institutions to explain their response to its recom-mendations. This should provide a source of political leverage, especially if the action or inaction of these institutions is made public after the summons.

It will be necessary, therefore, for this whole process to be institu-tionalized and made transparent from the inception of the Council. To this end, the Council's reports should be available to the membership of the General Assembly and the wider public.

In the longer term the Economic and Social Security Council, without veto power, should take on key decision-making roles in its areas of mandate similar to those of the reformed Security Council (see Part 1).

Committee membership should be on a rotation basis with each country having an equal vote. Election to the Council should follow the same basis as this report's proposals for election to a reformed Security Council.

Part 3

Global
peace and security

With the decline of the Cold War, the official ending of apartheid in South Africa, and the new possibilities for containing – and perhaps resolving – local and regional conflicts, the world seemed ready to usher in a new era of peace. Disarmament and arms control negotiations appeared more promising than at any time since the late 1940s. Multilateral institutions – both regional and global – were widely expected to play a key role in promoting a stable international order.

In this more constructive climate, it was hoped that states would rely less on the use or threat of force for the settlement of disputes and, that where conflicts threatened to erupt, the United Nations would take swift action either to prevent or to halt armed hostilities.

Boutros Boutros-Ghali's *An Agenda for Peace* was widely seen as a defining moment in the development of the UN's security agenda. Even though some of the Secretary-General's proposals exceeded the limits of what some member states were prepared to do, his pronouncements, and UN discourse and practice more generally, gave a new lease of life to pre- and post-conflict peacebuilding, peacemaking, peacekeeping and peace enforcement.

A great deal was certainly achieved during the 1990s, yet a depressing gap soon emerged between promise and performance. Over the last ten years, we have seen the continuing oppression of minority groups, rising civilian war casualties, soaring numbers of refugees and internally displaced people, the steady growth of the illicit arms market, and singular lack of will, especially on the part of the great powers, to rid the world of weapons of mass destruction.

After ten years of rising expectations and lost opportunities, it is time to take stock and redefine the agenda for global peace and security. In any future programme of action, the United Nations, by virtue of its mandate, experience and legitimacy, must be allowed to play a vanguard role, which is not to say that member states, regional organizations, non-governmental agencies and other institutions do not also have an important contribution to make.

In the proposals that follow we confine our attention to three major areas: disarmament and arms control; conflict transformation; and peacekeeping and peace enforcement. Before examining prospects in each of these three areas, we should, however, outline as clearly as possible the basic normative and operational principles that must guide the reform agenda.

GENERAL PRINCIPLES

The United Nations was founded in 1945 with the primary objective of achieving a more peaceful and secure world. Yet the environment within which the UN has had to operate over the last 55 years has not changed radically since the pre-1945 period. The world is still made up of a number of states, each of which claims the right to defend itself by military means. How, then, can the UN respond to this challenge?

The notion of general and complete disarmament, though the most appealing solution to the problem, remains at best a long-term prospect – which does not mean that important steps in that direction are unfeasible and unnecessary. It does mean, however, that if peace and security are to be pursued as realistic short-to-medium-term objectives (see 'Executive Summary' for a working definition of short, medium and long term), several key questions must be immediately addressed:

- How can states be prevented from using the force at their disposal?
- To what extent, if any, should the UN consider using force in order to secure the peace?
- If the use or threat of force by the UN is ethically justifiable, in what circumstances can it be applied?
- What specific strategies should it pursue?
- What are the most appropriate means?
- By whose authority should such decisions be made?
- Which institutions and mechanisms are best equipped to implement them?

To help us think through the maze of these complex questions, it may be useful to divide the UN's activities in the field of peace and security into two broad categories: those that exclude coercion as an option, and those that involve or at least allow the use or threat of force. In this sense, the deployment of military personnel as a buffer between warring parties qualifies as coercion, even if the forces deployed are used only for deterrence.

The UN's non-coercive peace efforts comprise disarmament and arms control, preventive diplomacy, peacemaking and peacebuilding, which are central to wider notions of *human, sustainable* and *democratic* security. The UN's coercive activities, on the other hand, cover peacekeeping and peace enforcement (including a variety of activities ranging from economic sanctions to outright collective security action).

To be successful, both coercive and non-coercive strategies must, however, be solidly grounded in some conception of human security. The ultimate objective must at all times guide the strategy rather than the other way round. Moreover, the security objective must be people-centred rather than state-centred. The aim must be to enrich and protect the lives of individuals and communities; to reduce levels of individual and collective anxiety; and to make human lives materially and psychologically more rewarding. In this context, states are at best a means to an end, not an end in themselves.

The concept of human security is a welcome antidote to the traditional preoccupation with military threats and military responses. It is an amalgam of two powerful ideas, namely *common* and *comprehensive* security. The first idea simply refers to the inclusiveness of the security objective. The security of one community, one nation or one region cannot be achieved at the expense of another. On the contrary, the security of different communities, nations and regions must be seen as complementary and mutually reinforcing.

The second idea underlines the multidimensional character of security. It integrates military security with notions of economic, environmental, political and societal security. The idea of comprehensive security is gaining wider acceptance, as more people realize that trade rivalries, international debt, destabilizing financial flows, international pollution, drug-trafficking, large population movements and human rights abuses all pose serious threat to human security.

The question, then, is how to weave these large and complex problems into one all-encompassing security agenda. The answer lies in devising security policies that seek to reduce the level of insecurity felt both within and between states. More specifically, such policies must be aimed at containing or avoiding the kinds of polarization that lead to armed conflict. They must adopt a more holistic and global approach to the complexity of the world's major crises.

We are now in a position to identify a little more clearly the principles that must guide any serious reform programme.

Sovereignty. It is probably the case that the classical notion of state sovereignty can no longer serve as the only guiding principle of state conduct. An acceptable balance has to be struck between the rights of states to manage their own affairs and the powers vested in international organizations that have been entrusted with representing the interests of humanity as a whole. Modern technology has created a highly interconnected global system that may require from time to time the attention and intervention of the international community.

Power and legitimacy. To make the case for global responsibility is one thing; to determine how such responsibility is to be exercised is quite another. The dilemma facing all multilateral institutions, notably the UN, is that in order to have the necessary levels of legitimacy, they must – through their actions and policies – simultaneously satisfy the interests of the strong and the weak, the rich and the poor. In extreme circumstances, the United Nations may have no option but to intervene directly on the side of the poor and the weak.

Democracy. Decisions are unlikely to be both legitimate and effective unless those affected by the decisions have a say in making them. In the case of the United Nations, it means involving all member states of the General Assembly, but also a representative cross-section of social and economic actors. The UN must apply democratic principles of decision-making, more rigorously and imaginatively than it has done in the past, not least in the performance of its peace and security function.

Success in time. Peace and security are relative concepts. The measurement of success and failure is therefore also relative. Whether a particular action by the UN has been successful or not may not always be immediately apparent. It is necessary, therefore, to trace the consequences of any action (or inaction) over the short but also medium and longer terms. The important point to note here is that peace operations, sanctions, peacemaking and peacebuilding initiatives must be developed with both shorter- and longer-term horizons in mind.

Consent. The case for intervention without the consent of all parties may sometimes be strong, particularly when armed hostilities result in gross human rights violations and mass and indiscriminate killing. On the other hand, there must also be a deeply entrenched commitment to the principle of autonomy (a more meaningful notion than sovereignty), that is the idea that nations and communities are entitled to manage their own affairs. If in any given conflict, be it intra-state or inter-state, the UN is seen as taking sides, the net effect might be to tarnish its credibility and reduce its long-term effectiveness. All peace efforts should be planned, directed and executed so as to maximize local support.

Resources. A key question that has consistently bedevilled the United Nations is that of resources. As a general rule, international intervention should occur only when the necessary resources can be deployed to ensure the achievement of the desired outcome. Conversely, where UN responses are consistently undermined by inadequate resources, member states and other relevant actors must reassess objectives and means, and re-establish a more durable balance between the two.

Institutional reform. The global changes of the past ten years have made a comprehensive rearrangement of the entire UN system essential. Proposals for such change must carry sufficient merit to convince the doubters. Some changes will require constitutional revision, others will require changes to policy and decision-making arrangements, others still could be part of the continuing process of administrative reform.

A number of key operational principles follow directly from the preceding discussion:

- Global governance reform must make international decision-making processes more effective and efficient but also more legitimate and democratic. The reform agenda must formally adopt as key objectives and benchmarks of success three key principles: transparency of decision-making; extensive participation and consultation; and rigorous levels of accountability.
- The reform agenda must be governed by clearly stated long-term objectives. More easily achievable short-term reforms must conform to and promote longer-term reform principles.
- Peace operations and disarmament and arms control must be closely integrated with preventive diplomacy, peacemaking and peacebuilding (with sustainable development and human rights as guiding principles).
- CSOs operating at various levels – local, national, regional and global – and pursuing objectives and activities that are consistent with the UN Charter must be democratically integrated into all aspects of global governance, and play an active but accountable role in conflict transformation, conflict resolution, and post-conflict reconstruction.
- The UN must enhance the role of regional organizations, assist them to develop more substantial instruments for the performance of security functions, and establish more effective collaboration mechanisms.

Disarmament and arms control

Since the end of World War II innumerable attempts have been made to promote treaties and agreements for the elimination, reduction or limitation of arms production, transfer or deployment. Regrettably, progress in disarmament and arms control negotiations, despite promising developments in the late 1980s and early 1990s, has been painfully slow.

Though some headway has been made in global and regional cuts in certain key elements of military power (e.g. size of armed forces, intermediate-range nuclear weapons, landmines), there is a long way to go before the lethality of actual and potential conflicts can be reduced to tolerable limits.

To illustrate the range of options and concrete steps that could be taken over the next decade to advance the disarmament agenda, we focus attention on weapons of mass destruction and light weapons.

KEY PRINCIPLES

Recent events, both internationally and regionally, suggest that it is time for the UN to undertake a mobilization of government, non-government and academic organizations, and popular constituencies, in a concerted global campaign to lock all states possessing or producing nuclear, biological or chemical weapons into binding schedules for the freezing, reduction and elimination of their arsenals and production capabilities.

The particular significance of regional conflicts in the post-Cold War environment, and the increasing probability of parties to such conflicts resorting to weapons of mass destruction, mean that it will be vital for the UN to pursue the new disarmament agenda at both global and regional levels simultaneously. Failure to progress on one level will potentially unravel progress on the other. Several principles should guide the disarmament agenda:

- Disarmament and arms control negotiations should over 25-30 years aim for substantial global and regional, quantitative and qualitative reductions in the main elements of military power (force components, inventories of weapons systems, military personnel and spending), and place clearly defined, verifiable and carefully monitored limits on arms production and trade.

- All states possessing or producing nuclear, biological or chemical weapons should be locked into binding schedules for the freezing, reduction and elimination of their arsenals and production capabilities.

- Control of small arms must address security, humanitarian and developmental concerns.

- Sustainable disarmament must address the fundamental causes of violence and demilitarization, and peacebuilding must be made an integral part of development.

- Regional organizations must institute and fund measures to eliminate, or at least drastically reduce, illicit weapons-trafficking within the broader framework of development and post-conflict reconstruction.

Weapons of mass destruction

Nuclear weapons

The 1998 nuclear tests by India and Pakistan – coming so soon after the 1996 conclusion of the Comprehensive Test Ban Treaty, the 1995 agreement to extend indefinitely the Non-Proliferation Treaty (NPT), and the 1996 judgment of the International Court of Justice that nuclear weapons are illegal under almost all circumstances – appeared to defy international norms, and represented a major setback to the process of nuclear disarmament. The tensions between the two countries made the situation even worse.

The tests were, however, symptomatic of problems in the disarmament process. Neither the United States nor Russia had yet moved decisively to reduce its nuclear arsenal, and not surprisingly the other nuclear powers were reluctant to lead the way. There has been little progress in achieving verifiable deactivation of nuclear weapons or physical separation of warheads from delivery systems. The nuclear powers have failed to agree to the non-use of nuclear weapons against specific countries, or to agree not to use nuclear weapons as a first-use option.

The failure to make substantial progress in eliminating or even reducing nuclear weapons from the now expanded group of eight nuclear powers, and the failure to reach binding agreements on the control and elimination of the four most serious instruments of mass destruction (nuclear, biological, chemical weapons, and missile delivery systems) suggests that the international community is facing an arms crisis potentially as serious as anything encountered during the Cold War. However, there are signs that the UN, in concert with sympathetic governments and NGOs, may still have the power to bring about effective measures of control and disarmament.

First, India and Pakistan have shown some concern for world opinion and respect for international norms by committing themselves to a moratorium on further testing and to bilateral negotiations to prevent nuclear war between them. They may be persuaded to go further. Second, agreements to form nuclear-weapons-free zones (NWFZs) have now effectively denuclearized the Southern Hemisphere and large parts of the Northern. Third, the United States and Russia have agreed to try to implement the START Treaty. Fourth, progress has been made on a fissile materials treaty. Fifth, the success of the campaign to ban landmines has shown what can be achieved by a working alliance of NGOs and sympathetic governments. Sixth, the UN has established a new Department for Disarmament and Arms Regulation (UNDDAR), which is expected to enhance the UN's disarmament role.

Other developments suggest that progress is possible. The eight middle-level countries that formed the New Agenda Coalition in 1998 have called on the nuclear powers to give an unequivocal commitment to the speedy and total elimination of their respective nuclear weapons and to enter wholeheartedly into the disarmament process. The New Agenda was passed overwhelmingly by the General Assembly.

The progress already made in establishing nuclear-weapons-free zones in Africa, Latin America, Southeast Asia and elsewhere shows the importance of regional activity. The UN should encourage further regions to follow this trend and, when they do, to join in exerting the pressure of their entire region on the nuclear powers, and to work towards treaties within their regions. There is progress towards such a zone in the Central Asian republics; even in the Middle East, with the divisions that exist between Israel, the Arab states, and Iran, arms treaties are not as remote a prospect as they might seem. Even in those regional organizations which include nuclear powers there can be progress, beginning with agreements not to extend current nuclear installations.

INITIATIVES

Especially in the nuclear realm, the tensions at this critical time are largely between the eight nuclear-weapons states and the rest of the world. The former (which also represent about half the world's population and much of its wealth) are reluctant to give up what they regard as a key aspect of their military security; the latter must rely on the strength of their collective voice and the rightness of their cause, with the determined participation of the UN, to convince the nuclear-weapons states that disarmament will not put their security at risk. The UN will need to enhance its role in disarmament at global, regional and national levels, and enlist the support and commitment of sympathetic governments, as well as academic, non-government and popular constituencies.

Multi-track mobilization. A new upgraded UNDDAR, the Secretary-General, and the relevant committees and working groups of the General Assembly, must embark on ongoing first-track and second-track consultations on the objectives and strategies of an integrated campaign. All possible forums should be used to exert pressure. As with the anti-landmines campaign, simultaneous public pressure from NGOs and governments at world conferences, as well as citizen and grassroots activity, research and negotiation, can achieve considerable progress in persuasion.

Interested governments could at the invitation of the UN or at their own initiative, host New Agenda conferences seeking to expand the number of governments committed to securing a nuclear-free world, to developing and implementing multi-track strategies of mobilization, and to developing model disarmament agreements.

Joint UN-regional organization partnerships. A more effective partnership should be developed with regional organizations to implement regional disarmament and arms control measures that can serve as stepping stones towards universal disarmament, particularly regional treaties and conventions that prohibit nuclear, chemical and biological weapons, and missile delivery systems, as well as implement regional verification systems and agreements on strategic doctrines; the processes and structures of this partnership would vary according to the particular characteristics of the regional body, the region's current disarmament and arms control issues and agendas, and its specific history and conditions.

Permanent Forum of NWFZ Treaty Secretariats. Meeting at strategic times, two or three times a year, such a Forum could seek to promote the consolidation and strengthening of existing zones, provide assistance to other regions contemplating zone establishment, liaise closely with UNDDAR and other UN disarmament bodies, share information and resources on verification processes, and promote more effective lobbying and international pressure towards wider disarmament objectives and strategies. Furthermore, a comprehensive study of zonal regional disarmament measures should be commissioned to update the UN's original 1975 experts' comprehensive study of nuclear-weapon-free zones.

The nuclear-weapons-free zone concept should be broadened to one of establishing zones free of weapons of mass destruction, free zones which would cover not only nuclear but also chemical and biological weapons; and to consider the question of also establishing missile-free zones.

Other steps. A first step must be unilateral or multilateral agreements to de-target and de-alert all nuclear weapons, and physically separate them from the means of delivery. Thus accidental nuclear war will be averted.

Further steps include: bilateral negotiations between the United States and Russia, proceeding on the basis of a rigorous timetable and committed to major START III reductions; multilateral negotiations involving all nuclear states, with a view to reducing their nuclear arsenals, and agreeing to an explicit timetable for the phased elimination of all their nuclear weapons.

Biological and Chemical Weapons

The problems of biological and chemical weaponry – particularly the former – achieved new prominence at the end of the 20th century. Continuing innovation in molecular biology and biotechnology is providing increasingly powerful ways to alter, control, and produce living things and toxins whose uses for weapons purposes are banned by the 1972 Biological Weapons Convention. Moreover, the knowledge and experience required to develop and produce chemical and biological weapons, once confined to a few states, will ultimately spread to all industrialized states. A current, acute form of this problem is posed by former Soviet bio- and chemical-weaponeers who developed the huge Soviet biological and chemical arsenals and who now seek employment elsewhere.

The security risks posed by the development, production, and distribution of biological and chemical weapons affect all states. However, in international settings, they are most often seen through the lens of the remaining superpower and its Western allies. Typically, the biological and chemical security problem is cast in terms of the 'self' that acts responsibly, even while retaining a huge arsenal of nuclear weapons (or protection under the nuclear umbrella), and the 'other' deemed to be hostile and irresponsible. Iraq and the Aum Shinrikio sect in Japan have become potent symbols of the threats posed by states and terrorist organizations. Furthermore, solutions are sought primarily through coercive, anti-proliferation mechanisms designed to deny access to information and materials or to disarm coercively to states that are seen as suspect. Meanwhile, leading Western countries remain silent on the question of seeking nuclear disarmament under Article VI of the NPT.

In contrast, the proposals below seek to express the concerns of all states and their citizens, in the South as well as the North. They emphasize a commitment to co-operative disarmament that encompasses all weapons of mass destruction, including nuclear weapons. They focus on achieving disarmament primarily through international reassurance and co-operation rather than through coercion.

INITIATIVES

The Biological Weapons Convention (BWC) and the Chemical Weapons Convention (CWC) should be seen as an important part of a global effort to abolish all weapons of mass destruction and, more generally, as precedents in a movement towards general and complete disarmament. All states should sign and ratify these conventions. Moves on the part of some nuclear states to use these conventions as counter-proliferation measures that rely for their effectiveness on resort to the threat, or even to the use, of nuclear weapons need to be challenged. Citizens should have access to the details of their country's policy positions so that these can be subjected to democratic examination and discussion.

Effective and equitable development and implementation of the **BWC** *and the* **CWC**. All states should adopt strong national legislation implementing these treaties without qualification and should participate in efforts to enhance compliance with them. No state should take executive or legislative action that dilutes implementation of these treaties.

Further development and implementation of the goals of the BWC and the CWC should be pursued in ways that ensure an equitable balance of rights and obligations so that these treaties do not benefit the richer, industrialized states at the expense of poorer, less industrialized states. Specifically:

- All state parties that are in compliance with the BWC and the CWC should receive equal treatment with respect to trade in dual-purpose agents and equipment covered by these treaties. The present activities of the Australia Group that affect state parties in good standing should be replaced by international export control standards established and implemented within the frameworks of the CWC and of the BWC Protocol under negotiation.

- The sacrifices made by poorer states to join and implement the BWC and its Protocol should be recognized and compensated through measures developed under Article X to share biological knowledge, materials, and technologies for peaceful purposes.

Transparency. To provide reassurance about their intentions both to other countries and to their own citizens and to ensure the effectiveness of the CWC and the BWC Protocol under negotiation, all countries should support high levels of transparency through declarations and inspections. In particular, the biotechnology, pharmaceutical, and agri-chemical industries should acknowledge that transparency for verification purposes should override interests in maintaining secrecy for commercial reasons. All states that have supported biological weapons programs in the past should declare them.

The roles of scientists, industry and institutions of higher education. Scientists, professional societies, research organizations, industries, and institutions of higher education should pledge not to engage knowingly in research or teaching that furthers the development or use of biological and chemical weapons. The development of novel biological and chemical agents that do not have unambiguously peaceful purposes should be prohibited, even if these activities are promoted for defensive purposes. All countries should develop legislation to protect whistle blowers.

Inspection regime. Any future inspection regime should be the responsibility of a United Nations commission under the UN Secretary-General. The inspectorate should be supported by the UN, not by individual member states. There must be strong procedural safeguards against the misuse of information by national governments.

International co-operation to contain terrorist interests in biological and chemical weapons. All states should co-operate in preventing acquisition by individuals or organizations of biological and chemical agents and materials that have no clear justification for peaceful purposes and that are not supported by the state for prophylactic or protective purposes.

Light weapons

Many analysts regard the political and humanitarian crisis caused by the proliferation of light weapons as the most important security and development challenge of the 21st century, but it has yet to come to the top of the global agenda.

Light weapons are weapons that can be carried by a person or a light vehicle. They include semi-automatic guns, machine guns, light mortars, landmines and hand grenades, and have caused most of the deaths or injuries suffered in post-Cold War conflicts. Their transfer is a global process, involving a web of arms traders, governments, individuals, brokers and criminal networks.

International market. While some progress has been made on the reduction of the various forms of heavy weapons, the proliferation of light weapons has expanded alarmingly. For example, between 1990 and 1996 the United States gave away surplus weapons to the value of seven billion dollars, including 200,000 machine guns. These arms find their way into arms bazaars and from there into the hands of guerrillas, terrorists and criminal organizations. Over the course of their functioning lives, these millions of cheap weapons circulate from one conflict to another. Often the distinction between legal and illegal weapons trading is hard to discern. This lack of transparency makes it doubly difficult to stop arms trafficking.

United Nations. The UN's Co-ordinating Action on Small Arms committee (CASA), set up in 1998, seeks to place light weapons issues within the broader peace and humanitarian agenda, and to co-ordinate UN action in the area. CASA has three priorities: an advocacy campaign to raise awareness of the problem; responding to calls for assistance from specific states; and the holding of international conferences on the arms trade. The UN's Group of Governmental Experts on Small Arms was also set up in 1998 to examine means of curbing the weapons trade and make recommendations for action.

Emerging codes of conduct. In the last few years progress has been made in the development of codes of conduct (primarily at the regional level):

- *Organization of American States.* The "Inter-American Convention Against the Illicit Manufacturing of and Trafficking in Firearms, Ammunition, Explosives and Other Related Materials" was signed in 1997 to promote co-operation among regional governments to eliminate illegal weapons-trafficking. Its weakness is that it does not affect national legislation 'of a wholly domestic nature'. Ratification of the convention has been slow, as it requires the passing of changes to each country's legislation.

- *European Code of Conduct.* In 1998, EU foreign ministers agreed to an EU Code of Conduct for Arms Exports. However, where there were contentious issues, the weaker option was chosen in each case. For example, countries are required to make annual reports on their arms exports, but not required to make them public. The Council of Europe and the Organization for Security and Co-operation in Europe (OSCE) have also developed codes of conduct.

- *Southern Africa.* The proliferation of light weapons-trafficking in Southern Africa requires determined, comprehensive and co-ordinated action at not only the local and national levels but also at the level of the region of Southern Africa. Since 1998, a general administrative agreement has been reached among the countries of Southern and Eastern Africa to strengthen government control over firearms.

- *The United States.* The US Code of Conduct requires the President to submit to Congress an annual list of countries that meet certain eligibility criteria for importing American weapons: democratic government, respect for human rights, non-aggression, and full participation in the UN Register of Conventional Arms. There is, therefore, an incentive for the government to press its allies towards incorporating these values.

INITIATIVES

These regional developments are only a small beginning. Apart from strengthening regional codes, the time has come to establish an international code of conduct, and an international framework which would co-ordinate all action against arms-trafficking, facilitate the exchange of information, prevent duplication, and ensure the effective allocation of resources. In this the UN must play a key role.

International action to prevent the proliferation of illicit light weapons should incorporate the following objectives:

- agreement on principles for regulating light weapons transfers and for reducing the demand for light weapons;

- raising public awareness about the dangers of illicit weapons;
- developing norms of civilian non-possession;
- restricting government-to-government trade;
- curbing illegal trafficking.

Towards an international convention. Ultimately the aim is to establish a binding international convention or treaty, whereby governments seeking to export weapons would be obliged to meet a number of internationally recognized standards. An international convention would also provide a framework for gathering information about the arms trade, and ensuring greater transparency in matters of arms production and distribution, legal and illegal.

More specifically, an international convention would address key issues of supply. It would:

- establish a clear distinction between the kinds of weapons that are legitimately available to military and law enforcement officers and those available to civilians;
- require strict state-based licensing arrangements for all weapons, and place limitations on the possession and use of guns by civilians. The licit use of guns and weapons would need to be registered with a public authority;
- ensure that all weapons are marked (showing, for example, the year and place of manufacture, as well as current ownership) so that records can be maintained and the movement of each weapon can be traced;
- establish regulations governing safe and secure storage of weapons, and provide training for their safe operation;
- impose effective controls over the export of weapons – exports would be permitted only where the recipient country observed democratic procedures and human rights, exercised civilian control over the armed forces, and was not engaged in armed conflict – to this end codes of conduct would be developed and applied by regional organizations and arms control regimes but with regional practices registered with and monitored by the UN.

In addition, the convention would:

- provide for a high degree of transparency in small arms management and control, including for the millions of small arms that are already in circulation;
- ensure adequate programmes for collecting and destroying surplus weapons;
- provide for evaluation projects and programmes for destroying light weapons in former conflict regions, such as former Yugoslavia;

- support law enforcement efforts in states where the illicit use of weapons is most severe.

Under UN leadership, a convention could be drafted with the support of sympathetic governments, relevant non-governmental agencies, and regional organizations – perhaps following the model of the Anti-Personnel Landmine Treaty. As with the landmine treaty, much of the monitoring and implementation would depend on NGO-government collaboration established in the run up to the convention.

The development of such a convention is only a beginning. If the ultimate aim is to deal with the causes rather than the symptoms of the problem, the factors contributing to insecurity and the demand for weapons (e.g. poverty, injustice and corruption) would have to be addressed.

Conflict transformation

As the 1990s drew to a close, there was increasing unease about the slow response of the United Nations, particularly when it came to preventing gross human rights violations, notably in Rwanda and Sierra Leone. Many factors contributed to the absence or slowness of the UN's response. For some the principal cause of the UN's failures had to do with its organizational deficiencies: 'overstretched and underfunded, bureaucratically and unimaginatively organized'; too many *ad hoc* decisions; lack of a coherent or systematic strategy for dealing with emergent conflicts.

It is particularly important that the UN acquires an institutional memory about what went right and wrong in different operations. There is a need to identify standard operating procedures and creative options in different types of conflict. Clearly, there is much that can be done better:

- more time for quiet post-hoc evaluations of UN interventions, including outside facilitation by analysts (to avoid the understandable defensiveness that internal evaluations sometimes engender);
- learning lessons in one sphere of activity that can be applied to or tested out in other cases;
- time for Chiefs of Mission, for example, to engage in reflective debriefing after UN operations;
- 'Lessons Learned' units to be established in the Department of Political Affairs and other relevant departments;
- exchanges between decision-makers and academics from the field, brain-storming the basic approaches to conflict management, de-escalation, trust development, conflict resolution, and war termination.

There is a need to examine how complementary, unofficial initiatives might assist the UN in resolving intractable conflicts. These complementary strategies, sometimes referred to as second-track diplomacy, are often able to generate responses to conflicts that elude official negotiators. Examples are the secret discussions between Israelis and Palestinians in Oslo in 1992-3 and President Jimmy Carter's visit to Pyongyang in June 1994.

KEY PRINCIPLES

- In devising an indicative global preventive action plan, the UN must adopt a multi-track new strategy, engaging and consulting with a wide range of social and political actors at all tiers of governance. At the heart of this reform programme is the concept of multi-track diplomacy. Neither first-track nor second-track diplomacy can encompass the full range of conflict transformation processes and techniques. Several types can be readily identified, beginning with the more obvious ones:

  - inter-governmental diplomacy at the United Nations;

  - governmental peacemaking through bilateral negotiations;

  - second-track diplomacy using unofficial forums such as the confidential Norwegian negotiations which eventually led to the 1993 Oslo Accords;

  - citizen diplomacy through private means – in the case of Somalia this might have entailed the use of traditional kinship networks by Somali tribal elders to moderate or resolve the conflicts;

  - economic diplomacy, including packages by donor agencies designed to sustain peace;

  - mediatory or other third-party intervention by CSOs (e.g. religious groups like the Quakers) with an established reputation for impartiality and conflict resolution skills;

  - diplomacy through women's movements, which, both at the local and international level, can mobilize women in conflict transformation processes;

  - communications diplomacy, with media-generated information and analysis helping to mobilize public opinion and mould the perceptions of policy-makers;

  - other forms of citizen diplomacy, including establishment of peace zones, peace corridors, and co-operation zones;

  - peace education and training programmes which address the root causes of conflicts and promote a culture of peace;

  - creative diplomacy using as intermediaries well-known artists and entertainers (e.g. Live Aid, Band Aid; and Comic Relief).

- There is more to conflict transformation than identifying relevant personalities, agencies and institutions. What is needed is the formation of an explicit coalition of willing states and non-state parties to breathe fresh life into the Charter's fundamental objectives. Only such a coalition is likely to legitimize the higher levels of strategic planning and co-ordination that must emerge between humanitarian and development organizations, human rights groups, humanitarian law agencies, military representatives, local and international peace groups, the media, business leaders, parliamentarians, municipal leaders, religious groups, scholars and artists.

INITIATIVES

Prevention, tracking and analysis. The UN's Department of Political Affairs has difficulty exploring emerging conflicts in the absence of a specific mandate for engagement from the Security Council. The Africa Division alone, for example, has had to cope with conflicts in Sierra Leone, and the Sudan, the continuing conflict between Eritrea and Ethiopia, not to mention ongoing problems within Liberia, Nigeria, Burundi, Rwanda, Angola, the Democratic Republic of the Congo and elsewhere.

For this, if for no other reason, there is a need to utilize a broader range of resources. Relevant national and international NGOs – both those dealing with conflicts generally (e.g. International Alert, Initiative on Conflict Resolution and Ethnicity [INCORE], International Conflict Initiatives Clearinghouse) and those with a more specific brief (e.g. Amnesty International, Human Rights Watch) – can make an important contribution. This is especially the case for mapping and researching emerging threats, reporting on these emerging threats and giving early warning of potential conflicts.

Independent experts, think-tanks and research centres can develop sound analyses of the origins and dynamics of different conflicts, while second-track conflict resolution practitioners might be able to design appropriate responses that will not alarm national leaders by raising the spectre of UN interference in their domestic affairs.

But more sophisticated early warning is useless without sufficient resources for early responses: for thinking and acting in time. More co-ordination is needed between the Secretary-General and the heads of UN departments in order to identify a range of preventive actions that can be applied before the problem is transferred to the Security Council.

Equally useful would be a pool of professional diplomatic and political personalities able to commit themselves on a long-term basis to undertaking good-offices missions.

Early warning and early responses to conflict require a flexible blend of strategies, from preventive diplomacy and conflict management to peacemaking, to peacekeeping and peace enforcement. The first three need to be given at least as much emphasis as the last two, because they address directly the structural sources of violence. These techniques should be applied and exhausted before a conflict crosses the threshold into armed hostility.

Peacemaking has to do with all the diverse methods that are used to restore and maintain the peace after hostilities have occurred. The application of provisions of Article 33 of the UN Charter – negotiation, enquiry, mediation, conciliation, arbitration, judicial settlement, resort to regional agencies or agreements – can be applied both before and after hostilities have taken place.

Perez de Cuellar and Boutros-Ghali both stressed the contribution that preventive diplomacy could make to confidence-building, early warning, preventive deployment and the creation of demilitarized zones.

Organizational reform. Other positive initiatives might include the following measures:

- strengthening the Office for Preventive Diplomacy and the High Commissioner for Human Rights;
- a more critical role for the UNHCR in developing lasting agreements, particularly in conflicts involving large numbers of displaced persons or refugees;
- greater use of the International Court of Justice to bring warring parties together, and of specialized agencies capable of applying economic assistance, using carrots as well as sticks;
- the establishment of a UN-sponsored *International Crisis Prevention and Response Centre* (ICPRC) directly accountable to the Secretariat, and having access to the resources of UN bodies but also those of member states, NGOs, think-tanks, universities and research institutes. Except in matters of vital national security, all state and non-state actors would be expected to co-operate with the UN in maintaining an extensive information bank. The Centre would provide regular public reports, serve as an early-warning system, and make assessments and recommendations for the Secretary-General's consideration. Where possible the ICPRC would be supported by regional crisis centres;
- periodic meetings (perhaps twice a year) of the Security Council to review actual or potential conflicts. These meetings could be held in the vicinity of the conflicts, and would attempt to identify what action the UN should take;
- the establishment of a UN National Office in *every* member state, in consultation with and with the co-operation of the relevant

government. Such an office would provide a point of co-ordination for *all* UN agencies and programmes in that country and report directly to the Secretary-General. One important component of each office's activities would be to contribute to the UN's early warning, fact-finding and conflict analysis capacity. Conflict transformation would be made an integral part of its brief;

- early establishment of an independent, well-resourced but accountable *International Criminal Court;*
- a heightened role for international financial institutions in long-term peacebuilding including conflict impact assessments for all major international economic and social development programmes;
- more direct and co-ordinated involvement of CSOs and regional organizations (e.g. ASEAN, the OSCE, the OAU, the League of Arab States, and the Organization of the Islamic Conference) in preventive diplomacy and peacebuilding programmes, including mediation and fact-finding missions to diverse conflict zones.

Peace operations

The UN's coercive activities in the field of peace and security include peacekeeping and peace enforcement, which together constitute what we call 'peace operations' in this report. Peacekeeping involves the deployment of a UN military and civilian presence in the field, with the consent of the parties, to implement or monitor arrangements relating to the control of conflicts, the partial or comprehensive settlement of disputes, and the delivery of humanitarian relief in situations of conflict.

Peace enforcement, on the other hand, is not predicated upon consent, and comprises all active measures of coercion, involving especially use or threat of force against one or more parties. However, peace enforcement need not always involve the actual use or even deployment of military personnel. Other forms of coercion or imposition of penalties, including economic sanctions or even severance of diplomatic relations, may be considered part of peace enforcement.

Peacekeeping has in recent years encompassed a much wider range of activities. On the one hand, it embraces notions of conflict prevention, including preventive deployment of large-scale forces, and various forms of support for civil authorities. On the other hand, it borders with peace enforcement, increasingly involving support for humanitarian relief operations, which may, for example, require military protection, establishment of safe havens, or demobilization operations.

Expanded peacekeeping operations have given rise to a number of grey areas:

- the distinction between inter-state and intra-state conflict has become increasingly blurred;

- consent is supposedly required of all parties to a conflict, but exactly what this entails in practice is not clear;

- much confusion surrounds the issue of force – how much may be used; how is it to be applied; given the complexity of the peacekeeping roles, the often-cited formula 'non-use of force except for self-defence' is proving less helpful than it used to be.

The UN's practice revisited

Several attempts have been made to trace the evolution of UN peace operations. Our periodization here builds on the works of Henry Wiseman and Betts Fetherston (see A.B.Fetherston, *Towards A Theory of United Nations Peacekeeping*, 1994).

The nascent period (1946-56). The first ten years of UN peace operations were in the main characterized by several small-scale observer and fact-finding missions. Most were short-term, although those set up in Palestine and in India and Pakistan still continue to this day to perform their tasks. The main UN peace operation of the period was the collective action in Korea, initiated and dominated by the United States (1950-53).

The assertive period (1956-67). This period saw the emergence of peacekeeping in the current sense of the term, beginning with the deployment in the Sinai Peninsula after the Suez conflict. In the mission to West New Guinea (1963-64), the UN assumed for the first time temporary authority over a territory. The mission to the Congo (1960-64), with its 20,000 personnel, represented the first major challenge to the conceptual distinction between peacekeeping and peace enforcement. In Cyprus (1964 to the present) UN civilian police were used as peacekeepers for the first time.

During this period the Security Council resorted for the first time to sanctions under Article 41. In 1963 it called upon member states to apply a total but voluntary arms embargo against South Africa. In 1966 it invoked Articles 39 and 41 to impose comprehensive economic measures against Rhodesia.

The dormant period (1967-73). The UN did not establish any new peace operations in this period.

The resurgent period (1973-78). Three missions were established in this period which corresponds to the OPEC oil crisis and its aftermath. All were in the Middle East: Sinai, the Golan Heights and South Lebanon. No peacekeeping mission was established outside the Middle East between 1965 and 1988.

The maintenance period (1978-88). Again the UN did not establish any new peace operations in this period, although it did continue its existing missions.

The transition period (1988-91). UN peace operations were revived in this period, beginning with missions to Afghanistan and to Iran and Iraq, once the conflicts had ended. In 1989 came the first sign of substantial change in the nature of UN peace operations, when a decade of obstruction by South Africa ended, allowing a UN mission to help Namibia's transition to independence. So-called 'multidimensional', 'second-generation' or 'expanded' peacekeeping in the post-Cold War period began with this mission. Three missions to Central America were notable for being the first UN missions sent to what had always been a US sphere of influence.

The enforcement period (1991-96). Iraq's invasion of Kuwait led to the second collective action in the UN's history: Operation Desert Storm. Three missions to the region followed; that assisting the Iraqi Kurds was noteworthy for challenging the principle of sovereignty and for defining a humanitarian crisis as a threat to international peace and security.

Other major missions established during this period included those to the former Yugoslavia, Cambodia and Somalia, each of which would become a more complex operation than any previous UN mission. In Somalia, the Security Council for the first time explicitly authorized a massive military intervention by member states in the absence of any invitation from the host state, and established a clear link between a humanitarian crisis and the use of force to restore peace and security.

In 1992 the UN imposed sanctions on Serbia and Montenegro and set up a mission to deliver humanitarian aid to Bosnia and Hercegovina. This mission had its mandate continually expanded in subsequent resolutions, prompting severe criticism of the UN's performance, notably by its own officials serving on the mission.

Large-scale military missions to Haiti and Rwanda were also established and completed in this period. The former was generally considered a success, the latter a disappointing failure.

The moderation period (1996-97). The difficulties encountered by the international community in dealing with the problems of Cambodia, Somalia, Rwanda and the former Yugoslavia severely eroded the enthusiasm for ambitious UN peace operations. Only a few relatively small-scale missions were authorized during this period.

The period of ambiguity (1998 to the present). Despite much activity by the UN, including personal intervention by the Secretary-General and condemnation of Iraq by the Security Council, Iraq failed to comply with UN weapons inspection requirements, and the United States and Britain launched a brief bombing campaign against Iraq in 1998. The UN had not specifically authorized this action.

Another development which signalled the bypassing of the UN peace and security framework occurred in 1999. In the face of what appeared to be the UN's failure to deal with the crisis in Kosovo, NATO decided to take matters into its own hands, and proceeded to wage an intensive bombing against the Federal Republic of Yugoslavia between March and June, which, among other things, resulted in the bombing of the Chinese Embassy in Belgrade. Following the cessation of the campaign and the withdrawal of Yugoslav troops from Kosovo, the UN established a mission there. Two aspects of the mission are worth highlighting. First, it has been vested with all legislative, executive and judicial powers in the territory it administers; second, it is so far the only mission in which other multilateral organizations (the EU, the OSCE, and NATO) are full partners under UN leadership.

More recently the UN has authorized a number of peace missions in East Timor, first a civilian mission – with the formal consent of the Indonesian government and assisted only by unarmed police – to oversee the ballot that resulted in a vote for independence; second, a multinational peace operation – led by Australia but again with the formal consent of the Indonesian government – charged with the specific task of ending, by forceful means if necessary, the militia-inspired violence in the territory; third, an explicitly UN operation – with a civilian and a military arm – charged with administering the territory (following Indonesia's decision to accept the result of the ballot) in preparation for full independence.

Equally significant have been the large-scale missions dispatched to the Democratic Republic of the Congo and Sierra Leone, both of which came to operate under Chapter VII mandates. At stake during this still unfolding period have been not only the UN's overall authority over multilateral peace operations, but also the very safety of its personnel.

Towards an assessment

What is particularly important from a global governance perspective is the relationship that has emerged between the United Nations and the various multilateral peace operations. Both during and since the Cold War the UN's normative authority over multilateral peace operations has been continuously challenged.

During the UN's first 40 years few peace operations took place. Extra-UN multilateral peace operations were even fewer. The challenge to the UN's authority had two manifestations. At times the major powers managed to get the organization to act in the way they wanted (e.g. the United States during the Korean crisis). At other times they shaped the UN's response by ensuring inaction (e.g. the Soviet Union during the Hungarian crisis).

In the post-Cold War period, challenges to the UN's authority were at first thought to be at an end. Yet before long it emerged that the challenge would continue unabated. By the late 1990s the full dimensions of the UN's authority crisis had become clearly visible. In the Kosovo crisis a Cold War alliance took independent enforcement action with almost no reference to the UN.

Evaluating UN peace operations is no easy task. Success or failure of individual missions is of course important, but not more so than the overall success or failure of the UN peace operations mechanism as a whole.

The crucial question is: What should UN peace operations be expected to accomplish, whether individually or collectively, for them to be considered successful? Success must be associated with the attainment of a set of identifiable objectives, which it should be possible to rank or categorize in some analytically useful way. The issue of success, and therefore reform, cannot be reduced to what might be termed 'operational' objectives. The purposes that UN peace operations, and at least by implication proposed UN reforms, are meant to serve are often treated as if they were clearly understood and universally accepted. This is a profoundly mistaken assumption.

To begin with, success and failure are relative judgements, which should be governed by two considerations. First, how closely the outcomes match the objectives that have been set; second, how adequate the chosen instruments are for the attainment of desired outcomes. These two considerations immediately raise two crucial questions: How can we measure whether the outcomes match the objectives? And, perhaps more importantly, does success depend merely on outcomes matching any one of a number of stated objectives? In other words, if there is uncertainty or confusion about the objectives, establishing appropriate processes or procedures becomes of secondary importance. An adequate evaluation of UN peace operations depends, then, on a number of key considerations.

Clarity of objectives. The foremost problem with UN peace operations has been the ambiguity of their objectives. This involves more than just the vague wording of formal mandates. It relates to the very rationale for multilateral peace missions. The relevant question is not whether a given formal mandate is clear enough, but what any multilateral peace mission should be designed to do. For example, was it appropriate for the UN to authorize a peace operation to restore democracy as it did in Haiti? The answer to this and similar questions is far from obvious, and merits closer attention.

Consistency. If success is a function of objectives, then the administrative and technical arrangements created to service UN peace operations machinery should be judged in large measure by the consistency with which the UN applies its standards. Similar diseases should be treated with similar therapies, subject to periodic and systematic review of therapeutic strategies and instruments. The particular dose or method of administering it may need to be tailored to the case at hand. However, in evaluating success, the choice of therapies and ways of administering them, important as they may be, must be treated as secondary to accurate diagnosis and consistently matching therapy with diagnosis.

Co-ordination, command and control. Global peace efforts should be co-ordinated through the United Nations. Here, the UN's authority and competence are key considerations. Even if the UN were considered to be no more than a policy instrument of states, the question would still need to be asked: What should be the UN's role in the authorization and management of multilateral peace operations? Is it, for example, acceptable that any regional or other organization should, as in the case of NATO in the Kosovo crisis, bypass the UN and proceed to use force without the explicit authorization and continuing oversight of the UN, however legitimate the cause may be?

Success in time. Any serious assessment of UN operations must take into account the time factor. Only with the passage of time is it normally possible to ascertain whether designated objectives have been met. Assessment of success cannot be frozen in time. It is itself a dynamic process subject to constant review. Conversely, if success is ultimately dependent on a long-term perspective, then it follows that, to be successful, any given peace operation must be integrated into a strategy consistent with the achievement of human security, which is in fact another name for the UN's larger peace and security mandate. To this extent, at least, peace operations must complement and dovetail with the UN's conflict transformation functions, notably preventive diplomacy, peacemaking and peacebuilding.

Recent reform proposals: discerning general trends

The UN's performance in the area of peace operations has come under wide-ranging scrutiny over the last ten years. A good number of academic and more policy-oriented reform studies – for example, the report of the Commission on Global Governance – have significantly contributed to greater public understanding of the issues. In this section we do no more than summarize the general tenor of these studies, highlighting a few key ideas and proposals which have provoked considerable discussion, and, in some cases, attracted a good deal of intellectual support. This is not to say that all or most of these ideas and proposals have been adopted by the UN system, or endorsed by its member states.

In reviewing some of the more important conclusions to emerge from these studies, we have chosen for purposes of analytical convenience to group them under four headings. The first three sets of conclusions relate to the major phases of any given UN operation: *assessment, authorization/ early planning,* and *implementation.* The last set focuses on *organizational reform.* It should be stressed that these conclusions, which we outline below, are not necessarily our own. However, as will become apparent, we use the accumulated wisdom derived from these studies as a building block for our more radical and extensive proposals.

Assessment (prior to making a decision)

Bringing conflicts to the attention of the international community. The UN needs a wide and efficient information-gathering capacity to identify potential problems before they become critical. To this end it should upgrade its existing capacities and establish co-operative arrangements with member states and appropriate NGOs.

Sending fact-finding missions or setting up special offices as close as possible to potential trouble spots can, in addition to increasing the UN's knowledge of the situation, draw international and regional attention to conflicts and act as a deterrent to armed hostilities.

Considering options and strategies. Preventive measures are paramount. Speedy preventive deployment of troops is a vital measure, but only when necessary and as a last resort, when other preventive methods – humanitarian aid, development assistance, mediation, diplomacy, sanctions – have failed. It is important to use the least confrontational method possible, for example, the good offices of the Secretary-General, or to involve an organization or group that carries no potential threat to the disputing parties.

Methods of intervention. When intervention becomes necessary it must be appropriate to the circumstances. Military force is a last resort, and even when used its action should be kept to a minimum – it may be that the very presence of troops will achieve the desired result. Other forms of intervention must have been exhausted first.

Sanctions of varying types and severity should be tried where possible, keeping in mind the effect of the sanctions on civilians within the target country and on others outside the target country. When sanctions are imposed, objective criteria for determining that their purpose has been fulfilled must be defined. Sanctions must be enforceable and designed to modify political behaviour, not to punish.

For the UN to be effective in complex emergencies, its different roles (military, political, humanitarian, development) must as far as possible be played simultaneously. The UN must also be prepared to follow each successful stage with appropriate action until a reasonable state of normality is restored.

Authorization / early planning (making the decision)

Consultative mechanisms. When the UN has decided upon military intervention, it could establish a consultative committee specifically for that operation, including representatives from each country contributing troops. It may also be desirable to establish a permanent body within the UN to prepare, and plan for, and to oversee, such emergencies.

Formal mandate. The goal of each operation must be clearly stated and translated into a precise mandate. Any change to that mandate must be approved by the Security Council and clearly stated. Ideally, any changes to a force's activities should be clearly allowed for in the original mandate.

Facing potential problems. When sanctions are imposed on a state, other states thereby confronted with problems should be able to have those problems satisfactorily dealt with. Also, countries that violate sanctions should themselves be subjected to sanctions.

On the composition of forces, it has been suggested that countries with special interests in, or historical association with a conflict should not contribute troops to a peacekeeping operation. The image, as well as the reality, of impartiality is essential.

The international community must be prepared to deal with the aftermath of its peace operations. On the other hand, it must also be prepared, when necessary, to acknowledge failure and withdraw, or at least change its mandate to one that is less ambitious and more achievable.

Resources. Quality, quantity and timeliness of the applied resources are all critical to the success of any intervention. The failure to achieve all three criteria has hampered many UN operations. The UN's resources in peacekeeping and logistical support may need to be significantly strengthened, and its ability to deploy them speedily enhanced.

The UN should keep a record of the resources that member states are able to contribute at short notice, and should encourage member states to keep a part of their forces ready to use should the need arise. It may be possible to identify the types of specialist personnel from each country who together could make up a force ready for immediate secondment to the UN according to the requirements of a particular situation. These forces would include not only military personnel but civilian police, diplomats, and human rights and other specialists. Equipment should be made available on a similar basis. The UN should co-ordinate training and information exchange among its prospective forces.

Implementation (after the initial decision has been made)

Initial / rapid deployment. Quick action is vital in the initial phase of operations. The UN should ideally have a force at its immediate disposal; whether this should be a dedicated permanent UN force or an enhanced form of the current *ad hoc* multinational arrangement is a matter of some debate. The permanent UN force would be more quickly and efficiently co-ordinated, but the political and economic feasibility of establishing such a force is open to question.

Command and management. The chain of command in a multinational force must be clear, unified and legitimate. The Security Council must maintain overall policy control, but in their current form UN forces should realistically continue under national or coalition command. It is vital that the boundary between the two is clear, as the integrity of the UN is paramount to the success of its operations.

Monitoring, reporting and reviewing. The UN Secretariat should have the capacity to gather, receive, analyse and disseminate information on the progress of UN peace operations, and do so on a continuous basis. Its monitors, including perhaps an ombudsman, should be clearly independent of other personnel.

Organizational Reform

One of the main weaknesses of the UN's operations has been its lack of organizational effectiveness. Various parts of the UN Secretariat, especially the Department of Peacekeeping Operations and the Office of Military Adviser, should be strengthened. The Secretary-General should establish and oversee bodies to integrate, co-ordinate and expand the UN's peace operations, taking under its auspices relevant sections of such existing bodies as the UNHCR and UNICEF.

The UN's peace operations could be decentralized into regions, as near as possible to the areas where the operations are to take effect. In addition, *all* UN operations in each developing country could be run from a single office.

Other international actors. Regional organizations and agencies possess a potential for working towards peace that has been under-utilized. Provided that the UN retains control over operations, it makes sense for those close to the area of trouble to contribute most to its resolution. They are likely to have more knowledge of their area and its problems, and have more to gain if a crisis is resolved and more to lose if it escalates. The knowledge that they will bear the burden of resolving problems also gives them an incentive to strengthen ties between them and their neighbours and engage in pre-emptive peacebuilding. They should also contribute more to early-warning capabilities.

NGOs also have an important role, particularly in working with the UN to develop early-warning mechanisms. Their political neutrality can give them wider access to parties to a dispute than the UN. Provided this neutrality is not compromised, they may perform several key functions in preventing, alleviating or mediating a conflict.

Peace operations: a reform agenda

Having considered the record of UN peace operations and discerned the general drift of reform proposals to have emerged in recent years, we are now in a position to spell out in broad terms an appropriate agenda for the future development of peacekeeping and peace enforcement.

KEY PRINCIPLES

Success in the conduct of UN peace operations is conditional on a clear understanding of the objectives that such operations must fulfil. To simplify matters a little we suggest a number of *primary* and *secondary* objectives. Primary objectives refer to desired outcomes specific to each conflict. Secondary objectives refer to more general outcomes, in the sense that they may enhance the prospect for success in many or all peace operations, or that they enhance the performance of the global multilateral system generally and the UN system in particular. Both sets of objectives are relevant to both intra-state and inter-state conflicts. Though in

An independent and adequately resourced *Impact Assessment Office*, accountable to the Secretary-General, should undertake the impact assessment. It should be able to draw on the resources of member states and NGOs, in addition to those of UN National Offices and the ICPRC, and it should report publicly from time to time during the course of the operation.

Formulation of mandate and complementary instruments. Ambiguity of mandates has hampered the effectiveness and the legitimacy of many peace operations. It is essential that mandates be clear. If force is to be used, then the purposes for its use, the amount to be used, the targets of its use, and the chain of authority governing its use must all be clearly stated in its mandate. A change to the mission should not occur unless the mandate has been explicitly changed accordingly.

A mandate should clearly state the mission's relationship to the parties to the conflict, and it should enshrine the principle of impartiality. It should also specify termination criteria – the social, political, legal or military conditions that should apply before the UN operation can be withdrawn or scaled down.

Deployment of human and material resources. For many reasons, some of them quite legitimate, national governments are often reluctant to commit military or other resources to peace operations. When they do commit such resources, co-ordination can be difficult, and valuable time may have been lost. For these and other reasons, there is now broad agreement that the UN's access to military and civilian personnel and logistic support should be greatly strengthened – either by the UN developing its own staff and equipment resources, or by member states placing more of their national capacities at the UN's disposal. Neither approach is likely to be easy or uncontroversial. In the short term the UN will probably have to rely on its member states, in which case the resources will need to be made available on a stand-by basis.

In order to make the system of national contributions more effective, the UN needs to build on its Standby Arrangements System, and further develop an extensive and detailed database on the resources each member state can contribute, their readiness, and any conditions that may apply to their use. It should also establish pools of appropriately trained military and civilian personnel who can be readily seconded – senior military officers, experienced judges and diplomats, senior police officers, and any others with appropriate expertise.

It should, moreover, be feasible for the UN to develop its resources in the short term. It could create a ready, portable stock of basic military equipment, and specific sets of equipment for the various types of operation it may need to undertake, especially for humanitarian relief. It could establish a permanent civilian police capability within the Secretariat, able to be deployed at short notice to trouble spots where full military deployment would be unnecessary, provocative or otherwise undesirable.

As the UN will still have to rely largely on the current system of national contributions for some time, it could set up a system of training for designated personnel from contributing nations, under an *International Peace Operations Centre*. This centre would eventually become the co-ordinating body for the UN forces which might be established in the longer term.

Mechanisms. The success of UN peace operations will depend on the adequacy of the available mechanisms, which are of two types: conflict-specific (those that are set up in response to the circumstances of a particular conflict) and general (those that have applicability to all situations). Peace operations must be supported by institutions and decision-making processes that are more inclusive, more transparent and more accountable than at present, but also more effective and efficient.

Every peace operation and its personnel (drawn from various contributing states and organizations) should be placed under the oversight of the *Strategic Committee*, which would report to the Secretary-General. This committee would replace the existing but moribund Military Staff Committee. It would gather the information and analysis necessary to submit to the Security Council a coherent set of proposals, and to ensure that the objectives set out in the mandate of peace operations are effectively acted upon. The committee would consist of one nominee from each member of the Security Council, and would consult as widely as possible with people with appropriate expertise. The Strategic Committee would also be required to engage in the widest possible consultation with the parties to the dispute. Its impartial control over operations would strengthen the UN's authority, especially in cases where a major power is involved.

For each peace operation the Secretary-General should appoint, on the advice of the Strategic Committee, an *Integrated Task Force* to be headed by his special representative. The task force would provide the necessary co-ordination between the military and civilian activities of the operation to ensure speed and effectiveness. It would also liaise with UN agencies and non-government organizations in the field; representatives of all such bodies should be co-opted as members of the task force.

Implementation

Initial / rapid deployment. The UN needs to have at its disposal a rapid reaction capability, under the control of the Secretary-General. This capability, multi-disciplinary in skills and functions, might be of modest size at first, becoming more substantial over the medium term. Made up of volunteer military and civilian personnel, the force would be trained by the UN's *International Peace Operations Centre.* The recent SHIRBRIG initiative by a group of like-minded states may help advance the conceptual framework for such a force.

In order to meet whatever contingencies may arise, there would still need to be stand-by national forces. Ideally these would form a multinational peace force, trained in accordance with the standards for the rapid reaction force.

Monitoring and reporting. The lines of communication between all elements of the UN's peace operations must always be open, and each element must have the capacity and the obligation to gather, analyse and disseminate information on a regular basis.

The Secretary-General, through the Strategic Committee, should be able to respond quickly to requests and recommendations from his Special Representative. In particular, human rights conditions in the host country should be constantly monitored, and any violations of human rights acted upon speedily. Every major UN field mission should be accompanied by an independent *Ombudsman*, whose primary function would be to monitor the conduct of the UN operation itself.

Organizational arrangements. The following initiatives are proposed:

- The *Force Contributors Committee* would function as a standing committee comprising one representative from each of the leading contributing nations. It would conduct a periodic review of peace operations and make recommendations for future improvements.
- The *Peace Operations Adviser* would act as chief of staff of the Strategic Committee. His office would advise the Committee on the state of potential conflicts, and on the military requirements of particular conflicts, should the UN decide to act. It would monitor the progress of peace operations.
- The *General Staff for Peace Operations*, located within the *Department of Peace Operations* (to replace the Department of Peacekeeping Operations), would be made up of fully professional and permanent personnel, both military and civilian, working within several units (e.g. military, police, human rights, electoral, administrative). It would service the UN's rapid reaction capability, monitor the readiness of national forces,

prepare and maintain contingency plans and operating procedures, establish training standards and co-ordinate admi-nistrative functions.

- The *International Peace Operations Centre* would recommend international training standards, develop training materials, mount training programmes, and keep a detailed record of the training activities of all contributing states.

- The *Force Contributors Panel* would function as an *ad hoc* committee for each specific peace operation. Comprised of one representative from each country contributing personnel to that operation, it would review its progress in consultation with relevant UN bodies and the Secretary-General.

Wider organizational reform

In the early part of this report it was recommended that the Security Council should be re-organized, the General Assembly and the Office of the Secretary-General substantially strengthened, and two new bodies established: a People's Assembly and a Consultative Assembly. Many of these proposed changes would significantly improve the UN's ability to discharge its responsibilities in the area of peace and security. Certain additional reforms specific to this function should also be seriously considered.

To make peacebuilding an integral part of UN peace missions, it may be useful for an inter-departmental peacebuilding unit to be established with direct access to the Secretary-General.

The Secretary-General should initiate a periodic review of existing regional security organizations, with a view to improving consultative arrangements with the UN, and increasing their capacity to collaborate with the UN on issues of peace and security.

At the regional level several initiatives should be considered depending on regional needs and circumstances:

- regional peace operations centres, which might oversee the preparation and development of training programmes;

- regional crisis centres, which could enhance early-warning and early-response capabilities in close co-ordination with the ICPRC;

- more effective liaison between regional organizations and regional arms of the UN system (e.g. the UN Regional Centre for Peace and Disarmament in Kathmandu).

- where it is proposed to delegate operational peacekeeping or peace enforcement tasks to a regional organization, the concluding of a formal agreement between the UN and the regional organization, setting out

Sponsoring institutions

Department of Politics, La Trobe University

La Trobe University, established in 1964, has grown to incorporate five campuses, and now has approximately 20,000 students and 4,000 staff. An international university, La Trobe has an extensive programme of links and exchanges with 65 universities in Asia, Europe and North and South America.

The Department of Politics, with about 20 academic members, takes a broad approach to the discipline and publishes outstanding scholarly research in a great many fields, but with a strong specialization in International Relations, Asian studies and Australian studies. The recent amalgamation of Politics with Sociology and Anthropology has further strengthened the capacity for research at the interface between these important disciplines, particularly around issues of globalization. As part of its international relations programme, the Department of Politics offers a wide range of subjects for undergraduate study, a graduate Diploma in International and Asian Politics, and supervision for postgraduate research at MA or PhD level. As of 2001, the department will offer a new Bachelor Degree of International Relations.

The Department of Politics also teaches at the Australian Defence College in Canberra, and publishes the scholarly journal *Pacifica Review: Peace, Security and Global Change*.

In 1995, the Department initiated a five-year research project focusing on the theme of Global Governance. As the first stage of this project it hosted a landmark international conference, *The United Nations: Between Sovereignty and Global Governance*. The conference, which featured workshops, panel discussions and more than 70 papers, resulted in a large number of publications, including A.J. Paolini, A.P. Jarvis and C. Reus-Smit (eds), *Between Sovereignty and Global Governance: The State, Civil Society and the United Nations* (London: Macmillan, 1998). The second stage took the form of six research fellowships awarded on a competitive basis in 1998. Several articles have since been published in Pacifica Review, dealing with such issues as democratic governance, genocide, and regional security. The present collaborative project on Global Governance Reform represents the third stage of the project.

Department of Politics, La Trobe University
Bundoora, Victoria 3083, Australia
Tel: 61 3 9479 2287   Fax: 61 3 9479 1997
Email: N.Mete@latrobe.edu.au
Website: www.latrobe.edu.au/www/socpol/

Focus on the Global South

Focus on the Global South was established in January 1995. It is based in Thailand and dedicated to regional and global policy analysis, micro-macro issues-linking and advocacy work. Focus gives priority to its work in developing countries, with a particular emphasis on the Asia-Pacific region.

Focus on the Global South is an autonomous organization, affiliated to Thailand's Chulalongkorn University Social Research Institute (CUSRI), and its sister organization is the Institute for Food and Development Policy in the United States. Focus is a non-profit organization supported by independent institutions and individual donors in both the South and the North. Able individuals and organizations are encouraged to contribute.

More specifically, Focus aims to:

- strengthen the capacity of organizations of poor and marginalized people in the South and those working on their behalf to better analyse and understand the impact of the globalization process on their daily life and struggles;
- improve critical and provocative analysis of regional and global socio-economic trends and articulate democratic, poverty-reducing, equitable and sustainable alternatives;
- articulate, link and develop greater coherence between local community based and national, regional and global paradigms of change.

Focus publishes a monthly printed bulletin of recent articles written by Focus staff, and two electronic bulletins, Focus-on-Trade and Focus-on-Security. Project and programme discussion papers, institutional progress reports and staff articles are available upon request.

Focus on the Global South, Social Research Institute, Chulalongkorn University
Wisit Prachuabmoh Building, Bangkok 10330, Thailand
Tel: 66 2 218 7363-5   Fax: 66 2 255 9976
Email: admin@focusweb.org
Website: http://focusweb.org

Toda Institute for Global Peace and Policy Research

The Toda Institute is an independent, non-partisan, and non-profit organization committed to the pursuit of peace with peaceful means and a complete abolition of war. In co-operation with other peace organizations that resist injustice and resolve conflict, the Institute aims at maximizing the efforts of people of peace of all colours and creeds everywhere. It is committed to principles of protection of all human life, safeguarding all of the natural environment, and harmonious development of all human communities, for which Josei Toda stood.

In helping to promote peace initiatives at national, regional, and international levels, the Institute encourages and proposes concrete strategies that can be translated into action. For the next few years, the Toda Institute is focusing on an international dialogue based on four major themes: (1) Human Security and Global Governance, (2) Human Rights and Global Ethics, (3) Social Justice and Global Economy, and (4) Cultural Identity and Global Citizenship.

In an effort to incorporate research into policy, planning, and implementation processes, the Toda Institute fosters dialogue among all four types of stakeholders (government, business, academic and civil society) by bringing them into interdisciplinary, transnational, collaborative, learning communities. It provides research, educational and advisory services on policy issues that critically affect the world community. Projects have already resulted in research, publications, and recommendations that can contribute to the resolution of world conflicts. Interpersonal as well as telecommunication networks are employed to organize international workshops, conferences, executive seminars and youth leadership development programmes, building for a more just and peaceful world.

The Institute publishes the journal *Peace & Policy*. Four volumes have already appeared in the HUGG Book series edited by Majid Tehranian et al. and published by I. B. Tauris in London: *Worlds Apart: Human Security and Global Governance* (1999); *Asian Peace: Security and Governance in the Asia-Pacific Region* (1999); *Not by Bread Alone: Food Security and Governance in Africa* (1999); *Nuclear Disarmament: Obstacles to Banishing the Bomb* (2000).

The Toda Institute for Global Peace and Policy Research

1600 Kapiolani Blvd., Suite 111, Honolulu, Hawaii, 96814, USA

Tel: 808 955-8231   Fax: 808 955-6476

Email: toda@toda.org

Website: http://www.toda.org